JIM BEAM

BOURBON COOKBOOK

JIM BEAM

BOURBON COOKBOOK

OVER 70 RECIPES & COCKTAILS TO MAKE WITH BOURBON

James B. Beam

NONE GENUINE WITHOUT MY SIGNATURE

An Hachette UK Company
www.hachette.co.uk

First published in Great Britain in 2018 by Mitchell Beazley,
an imprint of Octopus Publishing Group Ltd
Carmelite House
50 Victoria Embankment
London EC4Y 0DZ
www.octopusbooks.co.uk

ISBN 978-1-78472-330-9

A CIP catalogue record for this book is available from the British Library.

Printed and bound in China

10 9 8 7 6 5 4 3 2 1

Commissioning Editor Joe Cottington
Art Director Juliette Norsworthy
Junior Editor Ella Parsons
Senior Production Manager Katherine Hockley

Food Photography Dan Jones
Home economist & prop stylist Laura Fyfe
Designer Geoff Fennell
Recipe text: Charlotte Simpkins and Louisa Carter
Additional text: Justin Lewis

CONTENTS

INTRODUCTION

Any damn way you please.

That's how we recommend you enjoy Jim Beam® bourbon – and that sentiment is shared by our master distiller, Fred Noe. And as a seventh generation Beam, he should know.

You see, Fred is passionate about all things bourbon. From the basic ingredients to the way it's distilled, right the way down to the specific method we use for charring our barrels to get that unique flavour that's made our bourbon the number one in the world, enjoyed all over the globe.

And it's this unique flavour that's key in this book. Because although Jim Beam® makes for an undoubtedly fine drink on its own, it's when you begin to pair it with other ingredients that it can take you to a whole new level of taste.

Jim Beam® bourbon has an unmistakable flavour and aroma. It's bolder than other types of whiskey, with hints of smoke and caramel from our flame-charred barrels, and sweet vanilla notes that develop during the long years that it spends ageing until it's ready to enjoy. Combine this with undertones of oak and spice inherent in any good bourbon, and you have a versatile ingredient that can bring a whole heap of taste to just about any dish.

We've spent long hours in our kitchens coming up with a collection of recipes that really makes the most of our bourbon. From quick and simple dishes that deliver on flavour but can be knocked up without much fuss, to some crowd-pleasing centrepieces that are sure to go down well at barbecues or parties, we've tried to cover every occasion.

So if you're looking for an indulgent treat for a special event, you can try the *Eggs Benedict with Easy Bourbon Hollandaise* on page 26, the *Smoky Steak* with *Bourbon Butter* on page 72 or the *New York Bourbon Cheesecake* on page 140. For something quick and easy that's packed with flavour, go for the *Fully Loaded Black Bean Nachos* on page 50 or the classic *Kentucky Quarter Pounder* on page 79. Or if you're feeding a crowd, we've included some delicious recipes that you can scale up to suit your needs – look no further than the *Sticky Bourbon Wings with Asian Slaw* on page 42 or the *Pulled Pork Tacos with Sweetcorn Salsa* on page 60.

And you'll be very pleased to hear that bourbon and chocolate are a killer combination – to get your sweet fix turn to the *Bourbon Cherry Brownies* on page 122, the *Easy Chocolate, Bourbon and Raisin Ice Cream* on page 148, or even the *Kentucky Bourbon Chocolate Shake* on page 150.

The beauty of all of these dishes – and the others in the book – is that they showcase the huge range of flavours that are enhanced with the addition of Jim Beam® bourbon. From light fish and shellfish to big, beautiful joints of meat; from vegetables and side dishes to some truly decadent desserts, we've tried and tested them all, and have collected the very greatest here for you to enjoy.

And, of course, no collection of Jim Beam® recipes would be complete without some cocktails – so we've thought long and hard and brought together some of our absolute favourites. From stone-cold classics such as the *Old Fashioned* on page 176, to twists on some well-known drinks (check out the *Kentucky Manhattan* on page 174), there will be something here for everyone to enjoy.

So go ahead, flick through these pages and bring the taste of Kentucky to your table – we guarantee, you'll be pleased you did.

HISTORY AND CHARACTER

TWO CENTURIES OF BOURBON

For more than 200 years and through seven generations of the same family, we at Jim Beam have ensured that, in an ever-changing world, one thing remains constant: the process of how we create our finest Kentucky Straight Bourbon Whiskey.

Our secret blend of corn, rye and barley malt – known as our Mash Bill – is fed into a gigantic 10,000-gallon cooker. There, we add two crucial elements to the mix: firstly, limestone-filtered Kentucky water, iron-free and rich in calcium, and secondly, some 'setback' – some of the mash from the previous distillation.

We keep the content of our jug yeast secret, but it remains the same strain we've been using in our family business since the end of Prohibition in the 1930s. We mix the yeast with ground-up grain to create 'dona yeast', which is then combined in the fermentation process, where the mash is cooled to 15–21°C (60–70°F). The yeast feeds on the sugars in the mash, creating carbon dioxide and, crucially, alcohol.

Next, we heat the mash – by now known as 'distiller's beer' due to its similarity to beer in appearance, aroma and taste – in a 20-metre (65-foot) tall column still to 93°C (200°F), where it is vaporized and then liquidized. We go ahead and distil it for a second time in a doubler, where the vapour is condensed into something known as 'high wine'.

Once distillation has taken place, we make sure that this high wine is tapped into charred oak barrels, each of which can hold up to around 200 litres (53 gallons), to age and mature into the bourbon that we know and love. While the barrels are kept in storage, the changeable climate of Kentucky results in the barrel wood expanding, then contracting. Bourbon seeps into the barrel while the charred wood produces sugars, rich in both colour and flavour, with a caramelized taste. Meanwhile, some of the bourbon leaves the barrel through evaporation – we call the lost bourbon the 'angel's share' or 'Booker's share'. The whole process takes up to four years – twice as long as the law requires.

Our familiar mellow, smooth Jim Beam® flavour, popular around the world, has been painstakingly developed and perfected since the late 18th Century, thanks to seven hugely influential figures – all from the same family – who we now celebrate individually.

TWO CENTURIES OF BOURBON

THE SEVEN AGES OF BEAM

Jacob Beam (1760–1834) 'The Founder'

The origins of Jim Beam® whiskey stretch back to 1740, when the ambitious Boehm family arrived in the USA from Germany. The family changed their name to Beam, and by the 1770s the young Jacob Beam's father, Johannes, was one of the pioneering corn farmers in the Kentucky region of Virginia. In 1788, Jacob moved to central Kentucky, where a mild and warm climate and local limestone springs created the ideal conditions in which to grow corn. So much corn was grown that the excess was turned into whiskey, and in 1795, at the family distillery known as 'Old Tub', Jacob sold his first barrel of 'Old Jake Beam Sour Mash', made from his father's recipe. The new brand fast became a hit with pioneers, farmers and traders.

David Beam (1802–1854) 'The Pioneer'

Although Jacob Beam had established Old Jake Beam as a popular brand of bourbon, it was his son David who pioneered the brand's development. In 1820, David succeeded his father as the mastermind of the business, and under his watch the distillery expanded. More and more bourbon could be produced, as the distillery switched from the pot still to the more capacious column still and as production increased, the extra bourbon could be transferred, by train or steamboat, to locations beyond the confines of Washington County. In 1830, the business began using the charred wood of oak barrels, which previously stored fish or vinegar, to produce the sugars for the now-famous caramelized taste of its bourbon.

David M. Beam (1833–1913) 'The Visionary'

When David M. Beam took over the business, he became aware of plans to extend railway lines, and so in 1856 he moved the distillery to a location in Nelson County, which was practically next to the new rail lines. As a result, the newly renamed D.M. Beam & Co. could transport its bourbon both north and south. The brand was rapidly gaining national acclaim, and by 1861, its quality and popularity had even reached presidential circles. After it became known that the Civil War general Ulysses S. Grant was an 'avid bourbon consumer', his opponents confronted President Abraham Lincoln, accusing Grant of being a 'drunkard'. Lincoln reputedly responded: 'Find out what he drinks and send a case to my other generals.'

Colonel James B. Beam (1864–1947) 'The Colonel and the Legend'

It was James Beauregard Beam whose name would inspire the Jim Beam® brand. He took over the running of the distillery in 1894, by which time Old Tub® bourbon was well established as a national brand. Its secret recipe was of paramount importance, and Beam was protective of the contents of the yeast mix – he even took home a sample of the recipe to preserve the yeast strain. It is a strain that survives to this day. However, Beam's time running the distillery was interrupted in 1920 by Prohibition, and he abandoned the business. Fortunately for whiskey lovers everywhere, when the 18th Amendment was repealed in 1933, so ending Prohibition, Beam – now sixty-nine years old – began rebuilding the distillery in Clermont.

T. Jeremiah Beam (1899–1977) 'The Businessman'

It was James Beauregard Beam's son, T. Jeremiah, who helped him rebuild the distillery in 1933. They completed the task in just 120 days. By the time T. Jeramiah took over in 1946, not only had the revived Old Tub been renamed Jim Beam® Bourbon, but two new varieties had also become popular. Jim Beam® Rye was introduced in 1938, while the Mint Julep became the traditional drink of the Kentucky Derby. When he took charge, Beam initially oversaw the brand being shipped to U.S. servicemen overseas, insisting that no American should be without bourbon. To meet growing demand, a second distillery opened in Boston, Kentucky, in 1954.

Fred Booker Noe II (1929–2004) 'The Innovator'

Because Jim Beam's daughter Margaret had married into the Noe Family, her son Booker Noe II would oversee the next era of Jim Beam®. He became master distiller at the Boston Booker Noe plant. By 1964, bourbon was recognized by Congress as the U.S. native spirit, and the following year, production reached one million barrels. Noe oversaw a number of significant developments in the Jim Beam® story. In 1978, Jim Beam Black® was introduced, and a decade later, Booker's small-batch Bourbon collection began to appear – hand-made, uncut and unfiltered, using Jim Beam family expertise to produce some of the world's finest bourbon.

Frederick Booker Noe III (1957–) 'The Global Ambassador'

Fred Booker Noe III is our current master distiller. Not only does he champion Jim Beam® all around the world, he is also charged with preserving our secret recipe, and ensuring that every batch of Jim Beam® has that same inimitable flavour. Prior to taking charge, Noe gained experience in all stages of the bourbon-making process, having begun his duties on the bottling line. He even grew up in the same house, in Bardstown, Kentucky, as his great-grandfather, Jim Beam himself. He is the custodian of the secrets of Jim Beam® – taking 200 years of bourbon-making history and distilling it into every single bottle of Jim Beam® Bourbon.

THE SEVEN AGES OF BEAM

MEET THE FAMILY

The extended Jim Beam® family makes for quite a gathering – and every variety has a place in the kitchen. Though most of the recipes in this book are built around the classic taste of Jim Beam® Original, you can mix up the flavours in your dish by using different varieties of Jim Beam® Bourbon. From rich and full-bodied, to light and fruity, there is a variety to suit every taste, and to bring a different twist to many a dish.

Jim Beam® Bourbon

This is the original. Made with a special blend of corn, rye, malted barley, water, time and pride, Jim Beam® Original is the classic bourbon that people around the world know and love. A medium-bodied flavour, with mellow hints of caramel and vanilla, is reinforced by an oaky aroma with just a hint of spice. It's delicious, versatile and a sure-fire crowd-pleaser. Use this in recipes for that classic, can't-be-beat bourbon flavour.

Jim Beam Black® Bourbon

A smooth, elegant, refined drink, Jim Beam Black® Bourbon takes everything good about Jim Beam® Original Bourbon and turns it up a notch. Aged for years longer in white oak barrels, the flavours develop further to leave you with a full-bodied bourbon with a rich, heavy caramel flavour. An aroma of oak and vanilla lingers, with an undertone of cinnamon. This is the perfect partner for chocolate, or to finish off a dish with an extra punch.

Jim Beam® Double Oak Bourbon
finished in oak

Like all our bourbons, Jim Beam® Double Oak is developed in charred oak barrels. But its rich flavour comes from being aged a second time, in a separate barrel. The added interaction with the charred white oak results in a more intense bourbon, with toffee and caramel flavours, and rich notes of vanilla. Use this for barbecued meats, or to bring a light smokiness to cocktails.

Jim Beam® Rye Whiskey

Founded in 1795, our rye whiskey is made in the pre-Prohibition style. With its spicy, warm flavour, underpinned by the particular fullness of rye, it brings a spicy kick to recipes, with a black pepper bite. It has hints of vanilla and oak, but isn't as sweet as traditional bourbon, so is better suited to savoury dishes – though it can be used to tone down the sweetness of a dessert if you prefer a more savoury flavour.

Jim Beam® Apple
Apple Liqueur infused with Bourbon

Infused with premium bourbon, this sweet apple liqueur is perfect for bringing a light, sweet taste to a dish. Though underpinned with a fresh, crisp, green apple flavour, it retains the subtle oak undertones of bourbon. As you might expect, it works well in any apple dessert, but it's also perfect in fruitier cocktails, and pairs wonderfully with sweeter flavours such as maple syrup or honey.

Jim Beam® Honey
Honey Liqueur infused with Bourbon

One of the most versatile members of the Jim Beam® family, this is a great bottle to have to hand in the kitchen. Made by taking real golden honey liqueur and infusing it with our Kentucky Straight Bourbon, it contains complex notes of caramel, oak, vanilla and a finish of sweet honey. It'll pair well with shellfish, is a great addition to salad dressings and brings out the best in meaty dishes.

Jim Beam® Vanilla
Vanilla Liqueur infused with Bourbon

Made by combining the natural flavour of Madagascar Bourbon Vanilla bean liqueur with our bourbon whiskey, Jim Beam® Vanilla has a beautiful balance of rich, full-bodied vanilla with subtle hints of oak, combined with deep, caramel notes. It's best to avoid using this in savoury dishes, and instead focus on its ability to bring an added twist to fruity desserts, or any dish with chocolate.

Red Stag by Jim Beam®
Black Cherry Liqueur infused with Bourbon

An infusion of black cherry liqueur with bourbon whiskey brings Red Stag by Jim Beam® a soft, dark black cherry aroma, backed with a traditional bourbon oak. Characterized by vanilla, oak and caramel, its cherry sweetness is tempered by the smooth bourbon notes. Warm and smooth, it's a great option for adding a fruity finish to a cocktail without overpowering the other ingredients.

STARTERS AND LIGHT BITES

STARTERS AND LIGHT BITES

24 — BUTTERMILK PANCAKES AND BACON WITH BOURBON SYRUP

26 — EGGS BENEDICT WITH EASY BOURBON HOLLANDAISE

28 — BUTTERNUT SQUASH SOUP WITH CHILLI PEANUTS

30 — SMOKED SALMON WITH PICKLED VEGETABLES

33 — SPICY PRAWN COCKTAIL

34 — COBB SALAD WITH BLUE CHEESE BOURBON DRESSING

36 — WATERCRESS AND FETA SALAD WITH HONEY DRESSING

Buttermilk Pancakes and Bacon with Bourbon Syrup

Give this classic breakfast dish an indulgent twist by making a sweet, sticky bourbon syrup to pour over a stack of pancakes and salty bacon. You'll be guaranteed to have folks lining up for seconds – at any time of day.

SERVES 4

250g (9oz) or 12 smoked streaky bacon rashers

For the bourbon syrup
150g (5½oz) soft brown sugar
110g (4oz) unsalted butter
4 tablespoons Jim Beam® Bourbon

For the pancakes
200g (7oz) self-raising flour
pinch of salt
2 tablespoons bourbon syrup (see above)
250ml (9fl oz) buttermilk, plus extra to loosen
1 large egg
3 teaspoons rapeseed oil

★ Make the bourbon syrup first. Heat the sugar, butter and bourbon in a small saucepan set over a medium heat until the mixture is bubbling, then immediately reduce the heat to the lowest setting and simmer gently for 5–10 minutes. Remove the pan from the heat and set aside. The mixture will thicken as it cools.

★ Preheat the grill on a high setting. Grill the bacon for a few minutes on each side, until crispy.

★ To make the pancakes, put the flour into a wide, shallow bowl and stir through the salt. In a separate bowl, stir 2 tablespoons of the bourbon syrup into the buttermilk, then add the egg and whisk together well by hand. Pour the mixture into the flour and mix gently, stirring as little as possible, to produce a thick, lumpy batter. Add a splash more buttermilk to loosen the batter.

★ You'll cook 12 pancakes in 3 batches, so select a suitable large nonstick frying pan that will allow you to cook 4 pancakes simultaneously. Divide the batter into 12 equal portions. Heat the pan over a medium-high heat and swirl 1 teaspoon oil across the base, then add 4 portions of batter to the hot pan and flatten them out. Cook for about 1 minute, until small holes appear across the surface of each pancake, then turn them over and cook for a further minute, until cooked through. Transfer the pancakes to a warmed plate and keep warm while you cook the remaining pancakes in the same way.

★ Serve 3 pancakes and 3 bacon rashers per person. Drizzle over the cooled syrup to taste.

Eggs Benedict with Easy Bourbon Hollandaise

Lacing a creamy Hollandaise sauce with bourbon elevates Eggs Benedict to a whole new level. Hollandaise has a reputation for being tricky to make, but have no fear – this recipe won't let you down. Just keep the heat low when cooking the egg yolks, and make sure you take the mixture off the heat when you whisk in the butter. You can't go wrong!

SERVES 4

8 very fresh eggs

4 English muffins or bagels, split

butter, for spreading

160g (5¾oz) good-quality cooked ham (at least 8 thin slices)

1 teaspoon cayenne pepper

pepper

For the Hollandaise sauce

50ml (2fl oz) Jim Beam® Bourbon

2 tablespoons white wine vinegar

2 shallots, finely diced

1 tablespoon water

2 egg yolks

130g (4½oz) unsalted butter, melted and still warm

pinch of salt

★ To make the Hollandaise sauce, put the bourbon, vinegar, shallots and water into a small saucepan set over a medium-low heat and simmer for 2–3 minutes, until the liquid has reduced to less than one-third of the original quantity, so that 1 tablespoon of liquor remains. Strain the liquor into a medium-sized metal bowl, put the shallots into a separate bowl (to use as a garnish later) and set both aside.

★ Add enough water to a small saucepan to fill it to a depth of one-quarter. Set it over a medium heat and bring the water to a gentle simmer. Put the egg yolks into the metal bowl containing the liquor, set the bowl on the pan over the simmering water and whisk the mixture continuously for 1–2 minutes, until frothy. Now remove the bowl from the heat and whisk briskly while pouring in the warm melted butter in a slow stream to thicken the sauce. Season with the salt and set aside.

★ To poach the eggs, bring a wide saucepan of water up to a simmer over a medium heat. Stir with a spoon and then crack each egg into the water. Cook the eggs for 2–3 minutes, then drain on kitchen paper.

★ Meanwhile, toast the split muffins and spread with butter. To serve, top each muffin half with ham, a poached egg, Hollandaise, some shallots, a sprinkling of cayenne and pepper.

Butternut Squash Soup with Chilli Peanuts

Bright and vibrant, this soup will warm the soul on even the coldest of days. The chilli peanuts with a spicy hint make a nice crunchy addition and, if you like, you can garnish the soup with a handful of chopped coriander leaves for an extra splash of colour and fresh taste.

SERVES 4

1 tablespoon sunflower or olive oil

25g (1oz) butter

1 onion, roughly chopped

2 garlic cloves, finely chopped or crushed

150ml (¼ pint) Jim Beam® Bourbon, plus 2 tablespoons to garnish, plus a splash extra as desired

750g (1lb 10oz) peeled and chopped butternut squash

½ teaspoon mild chilli powder

750ml (26fl oz) vegetable or chicken stock, plus extra if needed

100ml (3½fl oz) double cream

salt and pepper

For the chilli peanuts

1 tablespoon sunflower or olive oil

25g (1oz) unsalted peanuts, roughly chopped

½ teaspoon mild chilli powder

★ For the soup, heat the oil and butter in a flameproof casserole or heavy-based saucepan set over a medium heat. Add the onion and fry for 5 minutes, until softened. Add the garlic and fry for 1–2 minutes, then pour in 150ml (¼ pint) bourbon and let the mixture simmer for 1–2 minutes. Stir in the butternut squash, chilli powder and stock. Bring to the boil, then simmer, part covered, for 20–25 minutes or until the squash is completely tender.

★ Use a stick blender to blend the mixture to a smooth consistency, adding a splash more stock or boiling water if you feel it is needed (if you do, heat the soup again thoroughly after adding the extra stock or water). Stir in the cream and heat through. Season with salt and pepper. You can add an additional splash of Jim Beam® at this stage if you want more of a kick. Keep warm.

★ For the chilli peanuts, heat the oil in a frying pan set over a medium heat. Add the peanuts and fry for 2–3 minutes, until just lightly browned, then stir in the chilli and cook for 1 minute.

★ Ladle the soup into warmed serving bowls and spoon over the chilli peanuts. Return the pan to the heat and pour in the 2 tablespoons bourbon. Bring to the boil and let the bourbon bubble for 5–10 seconds, before removing from the heat. Swirl the hot bourbon over the surface of the soup in each bowl and serve.

Smoked Salmon with Pickled Vegetables

Pickling an assortment of vegetables in bourbon and pairing them with smoked salmon makes for an attractive and impressive starter. You can get creative with the vegetables you choose – whole fine asparagus, shaved fennel, ribbons of courgette, sliced red onion, sliced radish, cubed carrot or diced cucumber all work well. The pickled vegetables will keep well for a couple of days if stored in a sealed jar in the refrigerator.

SERVES 4

3 tablespoons pine nuts

8–12 slices of smoked salmon

For the pickling liquor

1 heaped tablespoon white caster sugar

1 tablespoon distilled white vinegar

1½ tablespoons Jim Beam® Bourbon

½ heaped tablespoon fine table salt

1 tablespoon hot water

For the vegetables

1 small carrot, peeled and finely diced

1 small red onion, finely sliced into circles

8 pink radishes, finely sliced

1 small courgette, cut into ribbons with a vegetable peeler

8 fine asparagus stems

★ Mix all the ingredients for the pickling liquor in a bowl and whisk lightly so that the sugar and salt dissolve. Add the vegetables and mix well. Refrigerate for a few hours, then drain the vegetables and dry them on kitchen paper.

★ Put the pine nuts into a small frying pan set over a low heat to toast gently for 2–3 minutes, until lightly golden. Set aside to cool.

★ Arrange 2–3 slices of smoked salmon on each plate. Top with a selection of the drained pickled vegetables and a scattering of toasted pine nuts.

Spicy Prawn Cocktail

Pimp your shrimp with this easy, spicy, bourbon-spiked sauce, which works beautifully with the subtle flavours of the shellfish. Served with a no-fuss crispy green salad and a big chunk of crusty bread to mop up the piquant sauce, this tasty Jim Beam® version of a retro dish makes for a fun start to any dinner party.

SERVES 4

1 crisp lettuce heart (such as little gem or romaine), sliced

1 avocado, cut into small chunks

300g (10½oz) cooked peeled king prawns

1 teaspoon cayenne pepper

pepper

crusty bread, to serve

For the sauce

6 tablespoons Jim Beam® Bourbon

1 heaped tablespoon finely chopped red onion

1 tablespoon soy sauce

½ tablespoon tomato purée

200g (7oz) mayonnaise

½–1 teaspoon lemon juice

★ To make the sauce, put the bourbon, onion and soy sauce into a small saucepan set over a medium-low heat and simmer for 4–5 minutes, so that 1 tablespoon of liquor remains. Mix in the tomato purée, stirring for 1 minute, then take the pan off the heat. Pour the mixture into a bowl and set aside for a few minutes to cool to room temperature.

★ Put the mayonnaise into a bowl. Stir the cooled sauce mixture into the mayonnaise with lemon juice to taste.

★ Arrange the lettuce, avocado and prawns on a plate and drizzle over the sauce. Season with pepper and sprinkle with the cayenne pepper. Serve immediately with fresh crusty bread.

Cobb Salad with Blue Cheese Bourbon Dressing

SERVES 4

For the bacon and grilled chicken

1 tablespoon olive oil

2 teaspoons soy sauce

1 teaspoon Dijon mustard

1 garlic clove, crushed

2 boneless, skinless chicken breasts

8 smoked streaky bacon rashers

3 tablespoons Jim Beam® Bourbon

pepper

For the blue cheese bourbon dressing

4 heaped tablespoons soured cream

4 tablespoons mayonnaise

2 teaspoons Dijon mustard

125g (4½oz) blue cheese (such as Roquefort), crumbled

2 tablespoons Jim Beam® Bourbon, plus extra to taste

1 garlic clove, crushed

salt and pepper

For the salad

1 large or 2 small heads of crisp lettuce (such as romaine), chopped

200g (7oz) baby plum or cherry tomatoes, quartered or halved

4 hard-boiled eggs, shelled and sliced

4 spring onions, thinly sliced

2 avocados, diced

A big, hearty American Cobb salad is a guaranteed crowd-pleaser. Assemble the salad in the traditional style, layering the ingredients in rows on a platter, or throw it all together in a more casual mix.

★ First prepare the bacon and grilled chicken. In a bowl, mix together the oil, soy sauce, mustard, garlic and pepper. Add the chicken breasts and turn to coat. Set aside.

★ Heat a heavy-based frying pan over a medium-high heat and dry-fry the bacon for 2–3 minutes on each side, or until crisp and browned. Remove the bacon rashers and drain on kitchen paper. Add the chicken to the pan, reduce the heat to medium and cook for 6–7 minutes on each side, or until browned and cooked through. Pour in the bourbon, allow to simmer for 1–2 minutes, then turn off the heat and leave to cool.

★ To make the dressing, mix all the ingredients together in a bowl or jug, season with salt and pepper, and add more bourbon according to taste, if desired.

★ Assemble the salad ingredients either on a large platter or in individual bowls. Break the bacon into small pieces and arrange them on top of the salad. Cut the cold chicken into strips or cubes, toss in any pan juices and arrange the chicken next to the bacon. Serve straightaway, with the dressing on the side, or drizzled over the top.

Watercress and Feta Salad with Honey Dressing

The smoky-sweet flavour of Jim Beam® Honey works brilliantly with the saltiness of feta cheese – and the combination is even better when finished with a little kick of mustard and red chilli. This recipe makes a perfect vegetarian light meal for four, but this dish is also great as a big salad to serve on the side at a barbecue. Wait until the last minute to prepare and add the avocado, then pour over the dressing.

SERVES 4

For the dressing

150ml (¼ pint) Jim Beam® Honey

rind and juice of 2 oranges

1 tablespoon runny honey

2 tablespoons wholegrain mustard

2 teaspoons cider vinegar

2 hot red chillies, finely sliced

4 tablespoons rapeseed oil

salt and pepper

For the salad

200g (7oz) watercress, washed

260g (9¼oz) feta cheese

2 avocados, sliced

4 tablespoons chopped roasted hazelnuts

★ To make the dressing, place the bourbon, orange juice and orange zest in a small saucepan set over a medium heat and simmer for 5–10 minutes, until the smell of the alcohol has disappeared.

★ Pour this mixture into a large jam jar, add the remaining dressing ingredients, seal with the lid and shake well to combine. Taste and adjust the seasoning, if necessary, then set aside to cool.

★ Divide the watercress equally among 4 plates, then crumble over chunks of feta cheese. Add slices of avocado and spoon over the dressing. Finish each plate with a tablespoon of chopped hazelnuts.

Warm Chicken Caesar Salad

Try this warm and wintery take on the classic chicken Caesar salad. Once you try the bourbon-laced chicken breasts, it'll be hard to make them any other way ever again. Luckily, you won't need to, as they're incredibly versatile – just add them to any green salad to bring a smoky bourbon flavour to your dish.

SERVES 4

For the croutons

200g (7oz) ciabatta, torn into bite-sized pieces

1 tablespoon Jim Beam® Bourbon

3 tablespoons rapeseed oil

3 large boneless, skinless chicken breasts

1 tablespoon rapeseed oil

100ml (3½fl oz) Jim Beam® Bourbon

200g (7oz) kale, sliced

60g (2¼oz) shaved Parmesan cheese, shaved with a vegetable peeler

4 tablespoons Caesar dressing

salt and pepper

★ Preheat the oven and a nonstick baking tray to 180°C/160°C fan, Gas Mark 4.

★ To make the croutons, first put the chunks of ciabatta into a bowl. Pour the bourbon and oil into a small jar with a lid and shake well to blend, then pour the mixture over the bread and squeeze it into the chunks by hand. Tip the bread onto the preheated tray and bake for 12–18 minutes, until the croutons begin to turn golden.

★ Place the chicken breasts on a piece of clingfilm and cover with a second piece. Using a rolling pin or mallet, pound the meat to flatten it to an even thickness of about 1cm (½ inch). Season both sides of each flattened chicken breast with salt and pepper.

★ Select a large nonstick frying pan that has a lid and heat the oil over a high heat. Add the chicken and brown for about 3 minutes on each side. Pour in the bourbon and let it bubble for 2–4 minutes, then reduce the heat to the lowest setting, cover the pan with the lid and cook for 5–8 minutes until the chicken is cooked through. Switch off the heat and leave to rest.

★ Place the chicken and all of the pan juices into a wide, shallow bowl. Using 2 forks, shred the chicken into the juice.

★ Meanwhile, return the pan to the hob over a high heat, add the kale and cook for 3–5 minutes, until the leaves are wilted and most of the moisture has evaporated.

★ Layer the warm kale, Parmesan shavings, croutons and chicken onto warmed plates, then drizzle over the Caesar dressing to serve.

Jim Beam® Chicken Nuggets

A time-honoured sharing dish, chicken nuggets have a place on any table. In this recipe, the nuggets are marinated in bourbon before they're baked on a low heat, ensuring that the final dish stays moist and flavoursome. Serve with ketchup for dipping, or try the Bourbon Barbecue Dip on page 111.

SERVES 4

600g (1lb 5oz) boneless, skinless chicken breasts, cut into chunks

4 tablespoons plain flour

2 small eggs, lightly beaten

100g (3½oz) fine dried breadcrumbs

spray oil

ketchup, to serve

For the marinade

150ml (¼ pint) Jim Beam® Bourbon

1½ teaspoons soy sauce

★ To make the marinade, heat the bourbon in a small saucepan and simmer for 2 minutes, then stir in the soy sauce. Set aside to cool completely.

★ Place the chicken pieces in a wide, shallow bowl. Pour over the cooled marinade and toss to coat the chicken pieces thoroughly. Cover the bowl with clingfilm and refrigerate for 2 hours.

★ Preheat the oven and a nonstick baking tray to 170°C/150°C fan, Gas Mark 3½.

★ Remove the chicken from the refrigerator and discard the marinade. Place the chicken onto a plate lined with kitchen paper and pat with more kitchen paper repeatedly until each piece is thoroughly dry.

★ Put the flour, eggs and breadcrumbs into 3 separate wide, shallow bowls. Dip each piece of chicken first into the flour, then shake off any excess flour. Next, dip it into the beaten egg. Finally, roll it in the breadcrumbs to coat.

★ Spritz the preheated oven tray with a little oil. Arrange the coated chicken pieces on the tray and spray each piece with a little oil. Bake for 15 minutes, then increase the oven temperature to 200°C/180°C fan, Gas Mark 4 and bake for a further 5 minutes or until golden. Serve with ketchup.

Sticky Bourbon Wings with Asian Slaw

These tasty chicken wings are a great moreish snack, and the recipe is easily doubled or even tripled if you're feeding a crowd at a get-together. Fingers will get messy here, so a stack of napkins when you serve up is a must! Be sure to shred and slice the slaw ingredients as thinly as you can (you may want to use a food processor for this) to get a really fresh, crunchy effect.

SERVES 4

For the Asian slaw

1 large carrot (approximately 100g/3½oz), grated

100g (3½oz) white cabbage, finely shredded

1 small red onion, finely sliced into half moons

10 sprigs of coriander, leaves stripped

juice of 1 lime

For the wings

2 tablespoons Jim Beam® Bourbon

4 tablespoons sweet chilli sauce

20 chicken wings

1–2 tablespoons groundnut oil

salt and pepper

★ Preheat the oven to 240°C/220°C fan, Gas Mark 9.

★ Mix the slaw ingredients together thoroughly in a bowl and set aside in the refrigerator until needed.

★ To prepare the wings, first mix the bourbon with the sweet chilli sauce in a bowl.

★ Pat the chicken wings repeatedly with kitchen paper to dry them thoroughly, then coat well with the oil and arrange in a single layer on a large baking tray. Roast for 30 minutes.

★ Using a metal spatula, release the chicken wings from the roasting tray, then stir the bourbon and sweet chilli mixture into the baking tray to coat all the wings. Season with salt and pepper, then roast for a further 5–10 minutes, stirring halfway through, until the sauce is thick and sticky and the chicken skin blackens in places. Serve with the slaw.

Jim Beam® Piri Piri Prawn Skewers

The light flavour of Jim Beam® Honey pairs perfectly with sweet prawns and spicy piri piri sauce, but this recipe works just as well when made with Jim Beam® Bourbon. The marinated prawns are also delicious served cold on a simple salad.

SERVES 4

400g (14oz) raw, peeled (or with just tails) king prawns, defrosted if frozen

6 tablespoons piri piri sauce

2 tablespoons Jim Beam® Honey

1 tablespoon groundnut oil

pepper

To serve

1 fennel bulb, finely sliced or shredded using a mandoline

4 tablespoons lemon juice

1 lemon, quartered into wedges

★ If using wooden skewers, soak them in cold water for 30 minutes before using.

★ Pat the prawns with kitchen paper to dry them thoroughly.

★ Mix the piri piri sauce and bourbon together in a bowl, add the prawns, mix well and leave in the refrigerator to marinate for an hour or so.

★ Combine the fennel with the lemon juice in a bowl and set aside.

★ Prepare a barbecue to allow you to cook over a high heat, or set a griddle pan on the hob over a high heat.

★ Divide the prawns equally among the skewers and thread each prawn onto the skewer through both the tail and the body to prevent them from twisting. Brush each of the skewered prawns with oil and some of the marinade, and then season each side of the prawns with pepper.

★ Put the skewers onto the barbecue or griddle and cook for 2–3 minutes on each side, depending on their size, until all of the grey flesh has turned pink. Brush the skewers with more marinade as they cook.

★ Divide the skewers into 4 equal portions and serve with some fennel salad and a lemon wedge.

Prawn Burgers with Bourbon Mayonnaise

This is a sweet-and-spicy snack that can be whipped up without much notice using prawns straight from the freezer, as they defrost so quickly. To turn it into a more substantial meal, serve with homemade sweet potato chips and extra mayonnaise on the side for dipping, or Potato Wedges with Bourbon Barbecue Dip (see page 111).

SERVES 4

125ml (4fl oz) Jim Beam® Bourbon

3 shallots, finely chopped

1½ teaspoons soy sauce

100g (3½oz) mayonnaise

500g (1lb 2oz) raw peeled king prawns, defrosted if frozen

1 small garlic clove

pinch of salt

1 hot red chilli, finely sliced

4 brioche burger buns, split

2 teaspoons rapeseed oil

handful of peppery lettuce leaves (such as rocket)

★ Put the bourbon, shallots and soy sauce into a small saucepan. Bring the mixture to the boil, then boil for 2–3 minutes. Take the pan off the heat and set aside to cool, then divide the mixture into 2 equal portions. Mix one portion with the mayonnaise and set this aside. Set aside the remaining portion.

★ Place the raw prawns in a food processor with the garlic and a pinch of salt and pulse a few times until the mixture is coarsely combined. Tip it into a bowl and stir in the remaining cooled bourbon-and-shallot mixture and the chilli.

★ Divide this mixture into 4 equal portions. With wet hands, shape each portion into a patty – the mixture may seem wet and sticky, but it will firm up while cooking.

★ Toast the brioche buns lightly, then leave to cool.

★ Put the oil into a large nonstick frying pan that has a lid and heat it over a high heat. Add the patties and fry for 3 minutes on each side. Now reduce the heat to low, cover the pan with the lid and cook for a further minute.

★ While you are cooking the patties, spread the toasted buns with the seasoned mayonnaise. Once the patties are cooked, place one on the lower half of each bun. Divide the lettuce leaves into 4 portions and arrange on top of the patty in each bun, cover with the top half of the bun and serve immediately.

Fully Loaded Black Bean Nachos

Jim Beam® Bourbon adds just the right amount of smokiness to this easy black bean topping, which is always a hit piled onto a big plate of nachos and smothered with cheese. This is the perfect snack to serve up while catching up with friends and family – and meat lovers won't even notice it is vegetarian. Illustrated on previous page.

SERVES 4

200g (7oz) salted tortilla chips

4 tablespoons sliced jalapeños from a jar, drained

150g (5½oz) of your favourite melting cheese (such as Monterey Jack or Gouda), grated

100ml (3½fl oz) soured cream, to serve

For the black bean topping

1 tablespoon rapeseed oil

1 red onion, cut into thin wedges

½ teaspoon cumin seeds

1 fat garlic clove, finely chopped

pinch of salt

5 cherry tomatoes, halved

1 teaspoon chilli powder

50ml (2fl oz) Jim Beam® Bourbon

400g (14oz) can black beans, drained and rinsed

pinch of dried oregano (optional)

★ To make the topping, mix the oil, onion, cumin seeds, garlic and salt in a small, cold nonstick frying pan, then set the pan over a medium-low heat. Cook gently for about 7 minutes, until the onion is soft. Stir in the tomatoes and cook for a further 3 minutes, then mix in the chilli powder.

★ Increase the heat to medium, pour in the bourbon with a splash of water and boil for 1 minute, then add the black beans and simmer for 5–10 minutes. Now stir in the oregano, if using.

★ Preheat the oven to 200°C/180°C fan, Gas Mark 6 or the grill to a high setting.

★ Arrange the tortilla chips in an ovenproof dish and top with the black bean mixture, followed by the jalapeño slices. Sprinkle over the grated cheese. Bake or grill until the cheese has melted. Serve immediately, with dollops of soured cream.

Hot Dogs with Onion Chutney

This bourbon onion chutney is quick to make – but it's not for the faint-hearted. It's super-charged with bourbon, chilli and pepper, and is best served warm, smothered over your favourite hot dogs. Don't expect for there to be any left over! Illustrated overleaf.

SERVES 4

For the bourbon onion chutney

1 tablespoon rapeseed oil

350g (12oz) red onions, sliced into half moons

1 teaspoon sea salt flakes

1 teaspoon yellow mustard seeds

½ teaspoon chilli flakes

3 tablespoons soft brown sugar

50ml (2fl oz) Jim Beam® Bourbon

50ml (2fl oz) cider vinegar

pepper

For the hot dogs

4 big sausages or bratwurst

2 tablespoons of your favourite mustard

4 large hot dog rolls, split

★ Pour the oil into a large nonstick frying pan. Add the onions and thoroughly coat the slices in the oil. Set the pan over a medium heat. Once sizzling, stir in the salt, mustard seeds, chilli flakes and plenty of pepper. Cook for 5–10 minutes, until the onions are soft.

★ Reduce the heat to low, stir in the sugar and cook for 5 minutes to allow the sugar to melt into the mixture. Then increase the heat to medium, mix in the bourbon and vinegar and cook for 5 minutes or until the liquid evaporates. Switch off the heat.

★ Meanwhile, cook the sausages according to the packet instructions. Spread ½ tablespoon mustard over each hot dog roll and fill each with a sausage. Top with the warm bourbon onion chutney and serve immediately.

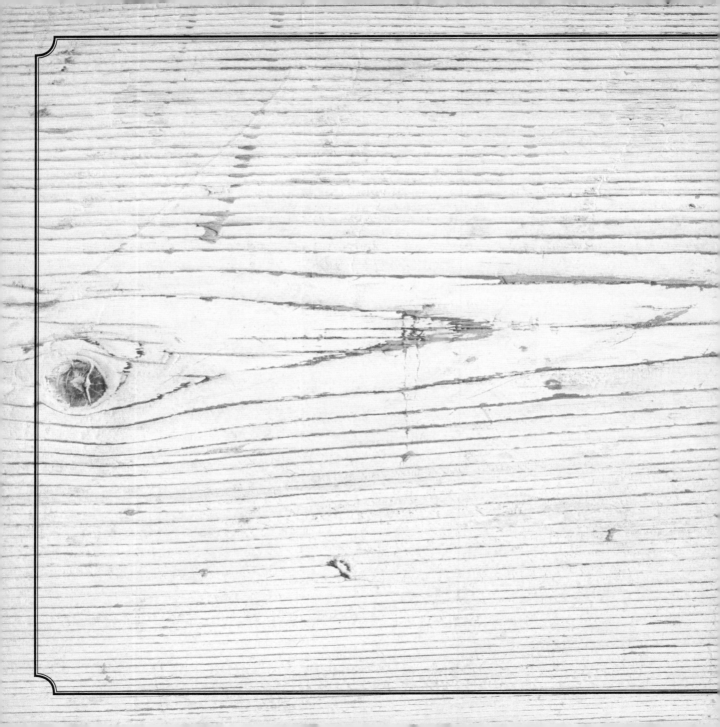

MAIN COURSES

MAIN COURSES

- (59) **PORK CHOPS WITH CREAMY BOURBON MUSHROOMS**
- (60) **PULLED PORK TACOS WITH SWEETCORN SALSA**
- (62) **BOURBON AND BACON RISOTTO**
- (64) **BOURBON BABY BACK RIBS**
- (68) **BEAM'S BAKED HAM**
- (70) **SPIKED CHILLI CON CARNE**
- (72) **SMOKY STEAK WITH BOURBON BUTTER**
- (74) **BARBECUE BOURBON AND HARISSA BEEF**
- (77) **SLOW-COOKED WHISKEY BRISKET**

Pork Chops with Creamy Bourbon Mushrooms

This dish makes something a little indulgent from the humble pork chop – it is served with a creamy mushroom and bourbon sauce and is perfect for a mid-week evening meal. Serve it with plenty of green vegetables and mashed potato for a hearty supper.

SERVES 4

4 pork chops, each 2.5cm (1 inch) thick (total weight approximately 900g/2lb)

1 tablespoon rapeseed oil

4 shallots, sliced

600g (1lb 5oz) mushrooms

100ml (3½fl oz) Jim Beam® Bourbon

75–100ml (2½–3½fl oz) double cream

salt and pepper

★ Preheat the oven to 160°C/140°C fan, Gas Mark 3. Set a large nonstick frying pan over a medium-high heat.

★ Brush the chops with the oil and season well with salt and pepper. Put them into the hot frying pan and cook for 5 minutes on each side, disturbing them only to turn them over once.

★ Transfer the chops to a roasting tray and roast for 10 minutes until cooked. Remove from the oven and leave to rest for a few minutes.

★ Meanwhile, make the sauce. Reduce the heat under the frying pan to medium and add the shallots to the pan. Fry for 1 minute, then add the mushrooms and stir to coat them in rendered pork fat. Season with salt and pepper. Add the bourbon and cook until the chops are cooked and rested. Reduce the heat to low and stir in the cream.

★ Serve each pork chop on warmed plates, covered with the mushroom and bourbon sauce.

Pulled Pork Tacos with Sweetcorn Salsa

A shoulder cut is traditionally used for pulled pork, but braising pork belly slowly in liquor creates sublime results – the meat just falls apart into the rich cooking stock. This dish tastes even better if made ahead and eaten the next day; just reheat it gently in a saucepan with a little water.

SERVES 4

1 tablespoon cumin seeds

1 tablespoon olive oil

1 red onion, roughly cut into wedges

5 tablespoons soy sauce

50ml (2fl oz) Jim Beam® Bourbon

2 tablespoons maple syrup

300ml (½ pint) water, plus extra as required

1.2kg (2lb 10oz) pork belly, skin removed, cut into 8 pieces as bones allow (reserve the bones)

12 soft or hard taco shells

For the sweetcorn salsa

160g (5¾oz) sweetcorn (drained weight)

½ red onion, finely diced

1 red chilli, finely diced

1 small bunch of coriander, leaves and stems finely chopped

juice of 1 lime

★ Preheat the oven to 180°C/160°C fan, Gas Mark 4.

★ Heat a small, heavy-based casserole pan over a medium heat, add the cumin seeds and toast for just 2 minutes, until fragrant. Add the oil and onion and cook for 5 minutes, until the onion is soft.

★ Switch off the heat, add the soy sauce, bourbon, maple syrup and measured water and stir to combine. Now add the belly pork pieces, ensuring they are covered in the liquid. Cover the casserole with the lid – you need a tight fit here to really lock the flavours into the pot, so if the lid fits the casserole loosely, wrap the lid in kitchen foil.

★ Transfer the casserole to the oven and cook for 4 hours, checking every hour or so and adding a touch more water if necessary. Remove the casserole from the oven and leave to rest with the lid on for 30 minutes.

★ Meanwhile, mix the salsa ingredients together in a bowl.

★ When the pork is rested, discard any liquid fat from the surface and remove all bones and any large chunks of fat. Using 2 forks, pull the meat into the remaining sauce and add a glug of water to loosen.

★ Warm the tacos according to the packet instructions.

★ Serve the warm meat inside the tacos, topped with the sweetcorn salsa.

Bourbon and Bacon Risotto

Traditionally, risotto is made with white wine, but for a simple twist, replace the wine with a good splash of bourbon – the results are delicious. As with any risotto, you'll need to stir the rice patiently throughout cooking, but the end result is rich and creamy – and well worth the time spent at the stove.

SERVES 4

1.2 litres (2 pints) chicken stock

2 tablespoons rapeseed oil

4 shallots, finely chopped

4 garlic cloves, finely chopped

4 celery sticks, finely chopped

300g (10½oz) smoked bacon, finely chopped

400g (14oz) risotto rice

200ml (7fl oz) Jim Beam® Bourbon

80g (2¾oz) Parmesan cheese, grated

handful of chives, finely chopped

40g (1½oz) unsalted butter, cut into small cubes

pepper

★ Heat the stock in a saucepan and keep it at a low simmer.

★ Put the oil into a large, shallow, heavy-based saucepan set over a low heat. Add the shallots, garlic and celery and cook gently for about 5 minutes, until soft. Increase the heat to medium, stir in the bacon and cook for a few minutes, until the bacon is cooked.

★ Add the rice and stir for about 3 minutes to heat the grains. Add the bourbon and stir until it has cooked away. Now add a ladleful of the stock and cook until all the liquid has been absorbed by the rice. Continue adding the stock, a ladleful at a time, ensuring all the liquid is absorbed by the rice between additions, until all the stock has been added. This should take 20–30 minutes. Add another 1 or 2 ladlefuls of water if the rice is not yet tender and cook until absorbed.

★ Stir in the Parmesan, chives and butter and serve immediately on warmed plates with a twist of pepper.

Bourbon Baby Back Ribs

This sauce is a marinade, cooking sauce and glaze all in one, so all of the awesome flavour is carried right through to the final dish. It's definitely worth marinating the meat if you have the time, but if you need a quick fix, you can skip this stage. Cook the meat in the oven, then finish it on the barbecue, if you can, for the ultimate rack of ribs.
Illustrated overleaf.

SERVES 4

1.5kg (3lb 5oz) or 3 racks of pork

100g (3½oz) tomato ketchup

For the marinade

50ml (2fl oz) Jim Beam® Bourbon

3 tablespoons dark soy sauce

2 tablespoons balsamic vinegar

2 tablespoons dark muscovado sugar

½ tablespoon tomato purée

1 teaspoon ground cumin

½ teaspoon mustard powder

¼ teaspoon smoked paprika

★ Mix the marinade ingredients together in a small saucepan set over a medium-low heat and simmer for 3–5 minutes. Set aside to cool completely.

★ Remove the thin membrane from the underside of each rack of pork and discard it.

★ Place one large food bag inside another to create a double layer. Add the ribs and marinade, squeeze out the air and seal the bags. Marinate the meat in the refrigerator for around 4 hours, turning the bag over occasionally.

★ When ready to cook, preheat the oven to 170°C/150°C fan, Gas Mark 3½. Place the ribs and all the sauce into a large roasting tray, cover tightly with kitchen foil and roast for 1½ hours.

★ If you are finishing the dish on the barbecue, prepare the barbecue so that you can cook over a high heat.

★ Once the cooking time has elapsed, remove the meat from the roasting tray and set it aside to rest while thickening the sauce. Place the tray on the hob over a high heat, stir in the ketchup and boil for 3–5 minutes, until thick.

★ If you are finishing off the meat in the oven, increase the oven temperature to 200°C/180°C fan, Gas Mark 6. Return the meat to the tray and brush over the thickened glaze from the tray. Return the tray to the oven and cook, uncovered, for a further 10–15 minutes or until the meat is done to your liking.

★ If charring on the barbecue, brush the racks with the glaze, place them on the barbecue and cook for at least 10 minutes, brushing the thick glaze over the ribs repeatedly while barbecuing.

Beam's Baked Ham

A glorious centrepiece for any gathering, this joint of ham is slow-roasted with bourbon liquor and then glazed with the bourbon cooking juices to give it a dark and delicious crust.

SERVES 4–6

1.5kg (3lb 5oz) smoked boneless gammon joint

150ml (¼ pint) Jim Beam® Honey, plus extra as required

1 heaped tablespoon wholegrain mustard

1 teaspoon runny honey

½–1 teaspoon chilli powder

★ When buying your ham, check whether or not it needs soaking prior to cooking. If it does, submerge it in water in a large bowl and leave it in the refrigerator for 24 hours. Drain the ham.

★ Preheat the oven to 160°C/140°C fan, Gas Mark 3.

★ Place the ham in a roasting dish so that it fits snugly. Pour the bourbon into the dish around the ham, cover the dish with a large piece of kitchen foil in one direction, scrunching the edges of the foil together, then use a second piece of foil to cover the joint in the other direction in the same way.

★ Cook for 4 hours, checking from time to time – if the roasting dish becomes dry during cooking, add another glug of bourbon.

★ Remove the ham from the dish. Pour the cooking juices into a small jug, diluting with a splash of water if very salty, and reserve. Carefully remove just the skin from the ham joint, leaving on as much fat as possible. Score the fat with a widely spaced criss-cross pattern. Increase the oven temperature to 210°C/190°C fan, Gas Mark 6½. Return the ham joint to the roasting dish.

★ Mix the mustard, honey and chilli powder together in a small bowl. Spoon one-third of this mixture onto the top of the ham and roast, uncovered, for 30 minutes, applying more glaze every 10 minutes. Leave to rest for 15 minutes, then serve with a little of the warmed roasting juices.

Spiked Chilli Con Carne

Bourbon brings a whole new depth to this crowd-pleasing dinner – and if you haven't tried adding a little dark chocolate into a chilli, then you really need to give this recipe a go. It may sound odd, but just try it – it adds a delicious richness. Serve with a dollop of soured cream, with rice or Bourbon and Chilli Cornbread (see page 114) alongside.

SERVES 4

1 heaped teaspoon cumin seeds

2 tablespoons rapeseed oil

2 red onions, chopped

pinch of salt

800g (1lb 12oz) minced beef

2 tablespoons tomato purée

1–2 teaspoons chilli powder

½ teaspoon sweet smoked paprika

200ml (7fl oz) Jim Beam® Bourbon

400g (14oz) can chopped tomatoes

300ml fresh good-quality beef stock

400ml (14fl oz) water

400g (14oz) can kidney beans, drained

20g (¾oz) dark chocolate, broken into pieces (optional)

salt and pepper

★ Heat a large casserole over a medium-high heat, then add the cumin seeds and toast for 1–2 minutes, until they release their fragrance. Then add the oil, onions and salt and fry for 5 minutes or until the onions are soft.

★ Add the minced beef, season it with salt and pepper and cook until the meat begins to brown and the moisture from the mince evaporates. Stir in the tomato purée, chilli powder and smoked paprika and cook for a further 2 minutes.

★ Preheat the oven to 170°C/150°C fan, Gas Mark 3½.

★ Pour the bourbon into the casserole and cook for 3 minutes, then stir in the canned tomatoes, beef stock, measured water and kidney beans, then bring the mixture to a simmer. Cover the casserole with the lid, transfer to the oven and cook for 2 hours.

★ Remove the casserole from the oven and stir in the chocolate, if using. Serve in warmed bowls with your favourite accompaniments, such as rice, lime wedges and soured cream.

Smoky Steak with Bourbon Butter

Try this dish for an awesome combination of flavours and the ultimate way to prepare a steak. You can make it indoors on a griddle pan or outdoors on the barbecue, but make sure you give each steak enough space during cooking – cook in batches if necessary. The delicious bourbon butter is all you need on the side.

SERVES 4

4 of your favourite cut of steak (such as rib-eye or fillet), at room temperature

For the bourbon butter

75g (2¾oz) slightly salted butter, at room temperature

1 teaspoon mustard powder

1 tablespoon Jim Beam® Bourbon

For the smoky paste

1½ teaspoons sweet smoked paprika

1½ teaspoons sea salt flakes

2 tablespoons groundnut oil

pepper

★ To make the bourbon butter, mash the butter with a fork until it is smooth, then mix in the mustard powder and bourbon and set aside.

★ Combine all the smoky paste ingredients in a shallow bowl and season with plenty of pepper. Set the steaks on a plate or tray and thoroughly coat each steak with the paste.

★ Prepare the barbecue to cook over the highest heat or set a griddle pan over a high heat. Sear the steaks on each side until cooked to your liking.

★ Smear or baste both sides of the steaks liberally with the bourbon butter. Leave the steaks to rest for 5 minutes, then top with any remaining butter to serve.

Barbecue Bourbon and Harissa Beef

A good-quality fillet of beef speaks for itself, but this ultra-quick marinade will bring out the very best in your meat, adding a hint of smokiness and a lick of spice from the harissa. Cook the meat on the barbecue to your liking, and serve it with some simple green vegetables.

SERVES 4

200ml (7fl oz) Jim Beam® Bourbon

3 tablespoons harissa

800g (1lb 12oz) beef fillet

★ Put the bourbon into a small saucepan, bring it to the boil, then simmer for 7–10 minutes or until reduced to a little over 3 tablespoons. Mix in the harissa and set aside to cool a little.

★ Place the beef fillet in a plastic food bag and pour in the marinade. Squeeze out the air from the bag, then seal it. Set aside at room temperature for 1 hour, squeezing the bag now and again to help the marinade penetrate the meat.

★ Prepare the barbecue to allow you to cook over a medium-high heat. Sear the fillet of beef for 1–2 minutes on all sides (about 8 minutes in total). Then reduce the heat of the barbecue by dispersing the coals a little, or by selecting a medium setting on a gas barbecue, cover with the lid and cook until the meat is done to your liking, turning half way through. The exact cooking time will depend on the temperature of the barbecue and the thickness of the beef fillet, but as a rough guide cook for a further 2–3 minutes for rare, 3 minutes for medium-rare and 4 minutes for medium.

★ Cover the meat loosely with kitchen foil and leave to rest for 10 minutes before serving.

Slow-cooked Whiskey Brisket

Homely and comforting, this dish is ideal for feeding a crowd. The recipe produces a rich bourbon gravy and a pile of buttered mashed potatoes. The potatoes are baked in the oven alongside the casserole, so are easy to make. It's definitely worth resting the brisket for around 30 minutes once it's out of the oven, to ensure the meat retains the delicious juices.

SERVES 4 GENEROUSLY

1.2kg (2lb 10oz) piece of beef brisket, boned, rolled and tied

2 tablespoons rapeseed oil

4 shallots, sliced

4 garlic cloves, crushed

350g (12oz) carrots, quartered lengthways, then cut into dice

2 celery sticks, halved lengthways, then thinly sliced

1½ tablespoons plain flour

150ml (¼ pint) Jim Beam® Bourbon, plus extra to taste

500ml (18fl oz) fresh good-quality beef stock

½–1 tablespoon dark soy sauce

2 bay leaves

2 sprigs of rosemary

400ml (14fl oz) water

sea salt flakes and pepper

For the mash

6 baking potatoes, skins pierced with a sharp knife

150ml (¼ pint) milk

30g (1oz) unsalted butter

sea salt

★ Remove the brisket from the refrigerator and leave it to rest for 1 hour to bring it up to room temperature. Pat the meat dry with kitchen paper and season with salt and pepper. Preheat the oven to 160°C/140°C fan, Gas Mark 3.

★ Set a medium casserole over a high heat and add the oil. When the oil is hot, add the brisket and brown it on all sides for about 15 minutes, then remove it from the casserole and set aside.

Recipe continues overleaf ➤——→

★ Reduce the heat to low. Add the shallots and garlic with a tiny pinch of salt and fry for 3 minutes, until they begin to soften. Now add the carrots and celery and cook for 3 minutes, then mix in the flour and cook for a further 2 minutes. Stir in the bourbon, increase the heat to medium, bring the mixture to the boil and boil for 2 minutes. Add the stock, soy sauce to taste, fresh herbs and half the measured water and bring to a simmer.

★ Place the brisket back into the casserole and cover tightly with the lid. Transfer the casserole to the oven and cook for 4½ hours, stirring occasionally.

★ After half of the cooking time has elapsed, put the potatoes into the oven, placing them on the oven shelf.

★ After the cooking time has elapsed, remove the casserole from the oven, lift out the meat and transfer it to a board. Cover loosely with kitchen foil and leave to rest while you make the gravy and mash.

★ Place the casserole on the stove top over a high heat and add a few more glugs of bourbon, if liked, along with the remaining measured water. Remove any woody herbs and simmer the gravy briskly until it has reduced to your liking.

★ For the mash, warm the milk and butter in a large saucepan. Meanwhile, wearing heat-resistant gloves to protect your hands, cut each potato in half and scoop out the flesh into the warm milk and butter mixture. Stir well and season with salt.

★ Slice the brisket and pour any resting juices into the gravy. Serve on warmed plates with the mash and lots of gravy.

Kentucky Quarter Pounder

This is an indulgent bourbon-spiked twist on the classic burger, complete with meltingly soft bourbon onions. Top it with cheese in a brioche bun and serve with skinny fries for a whole new way of enjoying a satisfying quarter pounder. Illustrated overleaf.

SERVES 4

For the burgers

450g good-quality steak mince

4 tablespoons fine dried breadcrumbs

1 small egg, lightly beaten

1½ tablespoons Jim Beam® Bourbon

½–1 tablespoon oil (optional)

4 slices of your favourite melting cheese (such as Monterey Jack or Gouda)

salt and pepper

For the bourbon onions

1 tablespoon unsalted butter

1 tablespoon rapeseed oil

2 white onions, sliced into half moons

2–3 tablespoons Jim Beam® Bourbon

To serve

4 brioche burger buns, split

shredded crunchy lettuce

ketchup and mayonnaise (optional)

★ To make the burgers, combine the mince, breadcrumbs, egg and bourbon in a bowl, mixing thoroughly by hand. Divide the mixture into 4 equal portions and shape each portion into a patty. Season both sides with salt and pepper and set aside to rest.

★ Now make the bourbon onions. Heat a nonstick frying pan over medium-high heat and melt the butter with the oil. Once frothy, add the onions and cook for 10 minutes, stirring occasionally, until soft. Add the bourbon and continue to cook until the onion slices are thickly coated and golden. Remove them from the pan with a slotted spoon and set aside.

★ Return the pan to the hob over a high heat to cook the patties. Add the oil, if necessary, and cook the patties for 3 minutes on one side, then turn, top each with a slice of cheese, and cook for a further 3 minutes, until the cheese begins to melt. Remove the patties from the pan and set aside to rest for 2 minutes.

★ While the patties rest, return the onions to the pan to heat through and gather flavour. Meanwhile, toast the brioche buns.

★ To serve, make a stack on the lower half of each bun with lettuce, a patty and onions, then top with the remaining bun half.

Barbecued Lamb Skewers

Don't be afraid of the anchovy in this marinade – it adds a deep saltiness that blends beautifully with the marinade flavours, and by the time the lamb is cooked there will be no hint of the fishiness at all. These skewers are great served with flatbread to soak up all the lovely juices, with a crisp, crunchy salad on the side.

SERVES 4

200ml (7fl oz) Jim Beam® Bourbon

3 garlic cloves, crushed

2 sprigs of rosemary, leaves stripped

1 tablespoon balsamic vinegar

1 small anchovy fillet, chopped

½ tablespoon rapeseed oil

650g (1lb 7oz) leg of lamb, cut into chunks

1 large red onion, cut into small wedges

pepper

To serve

4 flatbreads

crisp salad

★ Pour the bourbon into a small saucepan and bring to the boil, then simmer for 7–10 minutes or until reduced to a little over 3 tablespoons.

★ Reduce the heat to medium and add the garlic, rosemary leaves, balsamic vinegar and anchovy and simmer, stirring continuously, for about 3 minutes. Remove the pan from the heat, stir in the oil and some pepper, then set aside to cool a little.

★ Place the chunks of lamb into a bowl so that they fit snugly and pour over the cooled mixture. Transfer the bowl to the refrigerator to marinate for about 1 hour, turning the meat in the marinade once or twice.

★ Prepare the barbecue for direct cooking over a medium heat.

★ Thread the marinated chunks of lamb onto 8 metal skewers, alternating chunks of meat with wedges of red onion. Discard any remaining marinade.

★ Arrange the skewers on the barbecue and cook, with the lid closed, for 8–10 minutes, turning once, halfway through the cooking time.

★ Rest 2 skewers on each flatbread and serve with crisp salad leaves.

Baked Sweet and Sour Chicken Thighs

Spiking a sweet and sour sauce with bourbon is a quick, hassle-free way of creating a delicious supper dish. Bake the chicken thighs in a wide, shallow dish – giving each thigh a little space in the tray will ensure the skins crisp up perfectly. If you have time, allow the dish to rest before you serve. You'll lose a little of the warmth, but it will allow the flavours to develop beautifully.

SERVES 4

350g (12oz) good-quality sweet and sour sauce

5 tablespoons Jim Beam® Bourbon

8 chicken thighs (approx 1.2kg/2lb 10oz), on the bone and skin on

2 tablespoons rapeseed oil

240g (8½oz) white or brown rice

100g (3½oz) frozen peas

salt and pepper

★ Preheat the oven 200°C/180°C fan, Gas Mark 6.

★ Pour the sweet and sour sauce into a wide, shallow ovenproof dish and stir in the bourbon.

★ Rub the chicken thighs with the oil and season with salt and pepper. Arrange the thighs in the tray on top of the sauce and bake for 45 minutes.

★ Once the cooking time has elapsed, remove the tray from the oven and leave the meat to rest without covering for 5–10 minutes while you cook the rice.

★ Cook the rice according the packet instructions and, during the final 2 minutes of cooking, add the frozen peas.

★ Serve the chicken on a bed of rice in warmed bowls, with any sauce left in the baking dish spooned over.

Roast Chicken with Jim's Gravy

Once you try this method for cooking a chicken, you'll never go back. Bourbon is added to the dish while the meat roasts, steaming the flavour deep into the meat and making the most incredible gravy that's rich, dark, delicious and perfect for pouring.

SERVES 4

1 small carrot, roughly cut into chunks

2 celery sticks, roughly cut into chunks

1 red onion, roughly cut into wedges

2 garlic cloves, unpeeled

1 whole chicken, approx 1.75kg (3lb 14oz)

1 teaspoon rapeseed oil

100ml (3½fl oz) Jim Beam® Bourbon

50ml (2fl oz) water

1 teaspoon soy sauce

150ml (¼ pint) fresh chicken stock or water

salt and pepper

★ Preheat the oven to 220°C/200°C fan, Gas Mark 7.

★ Put the carrot, celery, onion and garlic into a medium-sized roasting tray and place the chicken on top. Cover the chicken skin in the oil and season with salt and pepper. Roast for 20 minutes.

★ Remove the tray from the oven and reduce the oven temperature to 200°C/180°C fan, Gas Mark 6. Pour the bourbon and measured water into the roasting tray, then return the tray to the oven and cook for a further 1 hour or until the juices run clear when the chicken is pierced. Remove the tray from the oven.

★ Lift up the chicken and tip the juices from the cavity into the roasting tray over the vegetables and roasting juices. Transfer the chicken to a plate, cover loosely with kitchen foil and set aside to rest while you make the gravy.

★ Place the roasting tray over a low heat on the hob and mash in the garlic cloves, discarding their paper skins. Stir in the soy sauce and chicken stock or water and simmer gently for 5 minutes. Strain the gravy into a jug, pressing the vegetables against the sieve to squeeze out as much of their juices as possible. Serve the chicken with the gravy along with your favourite accompaniments.

Duck Breast with Roasted Sesame Noodles

Duck breast pairs beautifully with bourbon-roasted vegetables in this smart dinner dish.
It's deceptively easy, too – the noodles and vegetables are cooked together in a zingy,
Asian-inspired cooking sauce. If you've never tried roasting noodles, give this recipe
a go; it brings out a range of textures, and they absorb the flavours of everything
they're cooked with.

SERVES 4

4 large duck breasts (skin on)

600g (1lb 5oz) pre-cooked or 'straight to wok' medium egg noodles

1 red pepper, sliced

3 fat spring onions, trimmed and halved lengthways

salt and pepper

For the dressing

juice of 2 limes

3 tablespoons soy sauce

3 tablespoons runny honey

2 teaspoons sesame oil

2 tablespoons rapeseed oil

1 tablespoon sesame seeds

50ml (2fl oz) Jim Beam® Bourbon

★ Season the duck breasts well with salt and pepper, then place them, skin-sides facing down, in a nonstick frying pan set over a medium heat and cook for 6–8 minutes, until the skin has a good colour and is crispy. As they cook, carefully spoon off the rendered fat and reserve it. Turn over the duck breasts in the pan, turn off the heat and leave to rest.

★ Preheat the oven and a large nonstick baking tray to 200°C/180°C fan, Gas Mark 6.

★ To make the dressing, combine the lime juice, soy sauce, honey and sesame oil in a small bowl or jug, then divide the mixture into 2 equal portions. Whisk the rapeseed oil and sesame seeds into one portion and set aside. Whisk in the bourbon and 2 tablespoons reserved rendered duck fat into the remaining portion.

★ Put the noodles, red pepper and spring onions into a large bowl, tip over the bourbon-laced dressing and toss thoroughly to combine. Tip the noodles onto the hot tray and roast for 10 minutes. Now place the duck breasts on the top of the noodles along with any juices from resting and roast for a further 15 minutes.

★ Slice the duck and serve on a bed of noodles, drizzled with the sesame seed dressing.

Bourbon-glazed Salmon Fillets

Just a few ingredients thrown into a pan are all it takes to make an awesome glaze for these salmon fillets – and it can even be made in advance if you're pushed for time. For an added twist, you can swap the Jim Beam® Bourbon for Jim Beam® Honey – just substitute the same amount, but reduce the quantity of brown sugar to taste.

SERVES 4

1 teaspoon fennel seeds

2 garlic cloves

pinch of sea salt flakes

4 tablespoons Jim Beam® Bourbon, plus extra to loosen

finely grated zest and juice of 1 lemon

2 tablespoons soy sauce

2 heaped tablespoons soft brown sugar

1 tablespoon rapeseed oil

4 salmon fillets (skin on)

★ Preheat the oven to 200°C/180°C fan, Gas Mark 6.

★ Using a pestle and mortar, crush the fennel seeds, then add the garlic and salt and crush together.

★ Pour the bourbon into a small saucepan, bring to the boil and simmer for 2 minutes. Add the fennel and garlic mixture, lemon zest and juice, soy sauce and sugar and simmer for a further 4–5 minutes. Once the surface of the glaze is covered in bubbles, set it aside to cool slightly and thicken. Add a splash more bourbon to loosen the mixture a little.

★ Put the salmon fillets on a baking tray, rub the flesh with the oil, then roast for 8–10 minutes, until pale all over and nearly cooked. Meanwhile, preheat the grill on a medium setting.

★ Once the roasting time has elapsed, remove the salmon from the oven and pat the fillets dry with kitchen paper. Brush the glaze onto each fillet and pour over any that remains. Grill for 4 minutes, until the glaze caramelizes and the salmon is cooked through. Serve drizzled with the melted glaze from the baking tray.

Pan-fried Fish with Burnt Whiskey Butter

Perfect for a smart dinner, this dish blends bourbon with pink peppercorns to make a sophisticated burnt butter sauce. It works well with just about any white fish, but try to find something thick and meaty for a sumptuous, luxurious meal. Avoid moving the fish too much during cooking, to keep it in one piece.

SERVES 4

For the potatoes

650g (1lb 7oz) waxy salad potatoes (such as Charlotte)

20g (¾oz) unsalted butter

handful of chives, finely chopped

pinch of salt

For the burnt whiskey butter

2 teaspoons pink peppercorns

50ml (2fl oz) Jim Beam® Bourbon

rind and juice of 1 lemon

80g (2¾oz) unsalted butter

salt

For the fish

2 heaped tablespoons plain flour

600g (1lb 5oz) white fish fillets (such as tilapia, mahi-mahi or cod), cut into 4 pieces

1 tablespoon rapeseed oil

salt and pepper

★ Put the potatoes into a saucepan of water, bring to the boil and boil for 15–20 minutes or until tender.

★ Meanwhile, prepare the burnt whiskey butter and the fish. To make the butter, crush the pink peppercorns using a pestle and mortar, then mix in the bourbon, lemon zest and half the lemon juice. Set aside.

★ Now prepare the fish. Put the flour onto a plate and season generously with salt and pepper. Pat the fish pieces dry with kitchen paper. Turn the pieces of fish in the seasoned flour to coat them, then shake off any excess flour.

★ Heat a large nonstick frying pan over a medium-high heat. Add the oil, then fry the fish for 2–3 minutes on each side until nearly cooked through. Carefully remove the fish pieces from the pan, loosely enclose them in kitchen foil and set aside to rest.

★ You'll use the pan in which you cooked the fish to finish making the whiskey butter. Wipe the hot pan carefully with kitchen paper and place it back over a medium-low heat. Add the butter. It will instantly melt and foam and, soon afterwards, turn brown and become still. At this point, stand back and add the bourbon, peppercorn and lemon mixture and let it bubble for 2–3 minutes, then remove the pan from the heat, taste and season with more lemon juice or salt, as necessary.

★ While the whiskey butter mixture is cooking, drain the boiled potatoes, cut each one in half and return to the pan, then toss in the butter, chives and salt.

★ Serve each piece of fish drizzled with the burnt whiskey butter and the potatoes alongside.

Harvest Chilli with Mixed Beans

A big, hearty chilli is a hard thing to beat, and this vegetarian version is a sure-fire winner. You can use cans of mixed beans, or mix and match any combination of butter beans, chickpeas, cannellini beans, kidney beans, haricot beans or pinto beans. Try to cut all of your vegetables to roughly the same size – it'll help everything to cook nice and evenly. Illustrated overleaf.

SERVES 4

For the chilli

2 tablespoons olive oil

1 large onion, finely chopped

2 garlic cloves, finely chopped or crushed

1½ teaspoons ground cumin

1 teaspoon sweet smoked paprika (optional)

½–1 teaspoon chilli powder

heaped ½ teaspoon ground cinnamon

100ml (3½fl oz) Jim Beam® Bourbon

2 red, orange or yellow peppers, chopped

1 courgette, chopped

1 sweet potato, peeled and chopped

2 x 400g (14oz) cans mixed beans, drained

680g (1lb 8oz) jar passata

1 heaped teaspoon soft dark brown sugar or muscovado sugar

salt and pepper

large handful of fresh coriander, leaves roughly chopped, to garnish

To serve

plain boiled rice (white or brown)

soured cream

grated mature Cheddar cheese

1 lime, cut into wedges

★ Heat the olive oil in a large flameproof casserole or heavy-based saucepan over a medium heat. Add the onion and fry for 7–8 minutes, until softened and golden. Stir in the garlic and fry for a further 2 minutes. Now stir in the ground spices and fry for 1 minute. Pour in the bourbon and allow to simmer for 1 minute.

★ Tip in all the vegetables, the drained beans and the passata. Roughly half-fill the passata jar with water and add it to the pan, then stir in the sugar and season with salt and pepper. Simmer, part-covered, over a medium-low heat for 30 minutes, stirring from time to time and adding more water if needed to stop the mixture becoming dry.

★ Taste the mixture to check the seasoning, then scatter over the fresh coriander. Serve with rice on the side and with bowls of soured cream, grated cheese and lime wedges.

Macaroni Cheese with Bourbon Crust

A warm, homely dish, spiked with bourbon-infused breadcrumbs for an added crunchy kick – what's not to love? If you're making this ahead of time, don't mix the pasta into the cheese sauce until you're almost ready to serve, to prevent the macaroni from becoming soggy.

SERVES 4

300g (10½oz) macaroni
568ml (1 pint) milk
40g (1½oz) unsalted butter
2 tablespoons plain flour
1 teaspoon mustard powder
100g (3½oz) Cheddar cheese, grated
generous pinch of salt

For the topping
130g (4½oz) ciabatta breadcrumbs
50g (1¾oz) Parmesan cheese, grated
1 tablespoon thyme leaves
50ml (2fl oz) Jim Beam® Bourbon
2 tablespoons olive oil
salt

★ Bring a large pan of salted water to the boil over a high heat. Add the macaroni and cook according to the packet instructions. Drain the pasta, rinse thoroughly, then set aside in a colander to drain further.

★ Preheat the grill and an ovenproof dish measuring roughly 20 x 30cm (8 x 12 inches) on the highest setting.

★ Warm the milk until warm (not hot) in a small saucepan set over a low heat, ensuring it does not boil.

★ Melt the butter in a large saucepan set over a medium heat. When it is frothy, add the flour and mustard powder, mix well and cook for 1 minute. Add the warm milk, whisking continuously, and continue to whisk while you cook for a further 3–5 minutes, until the mixture thickens slightly. Reduce the heat to the lowest setting and whisk in the cheese until the sauce is smooth. Season with the salt.

★ Add the drained pasta to the cheese sauce, increase the heat a little and mix thoroughly to combine and warm it through, ensuring the sauce does not boil.

★ Meanwhile, combine the topping ingredients thoroughly.

★ Transfer the pasta and cheese sauce into the warmed ovenproof dish and spread over the topping. Grill for 4–6 minutes or until the topping is golden and crunchy. Serve immediately.

Bourbon-roasted Vegetables and Cheese

This is a great, versatile meat-free main course for four that also works as a side dish with a difference for a group of six. It can be made in advance and cooled, to serve as a winter salad, and it reheats beautifully – just warm it slowly in a large, lidded pan with a good splash of water, and dress once warm.

SERVES 4

200g (7oz) small green/brown or Puy lentils

160g (5¾oz) soft goat's cheese or feta cheese

pepper

For the dressing

6 tablespoons Jim Beam® Bourbon

3 tablespoons runny honey

3 tablespoons soy sauce

finely grated zest and juice of 1 large lemon

½–1 teaspoon chilli powder

100ml (3½fl oz) rapeseed oil

For the roasted vegetables

2 carrots, thickly sliced

3 peppers of varying colours, cut into chunks

2 red onions, cut into thick wedges

200g (7oz) mushrooms, quartered

2 courgettes, cut into thick slices

1 aubergine, cut into chunks

4 fat garlic cloves, unpeeled

★ Preheat the oven and 2 large nonstick baking trays to 180°C/160°C fan, Gas Mark 4.

★ To make the dressing, put the bourbon, honey, soy sauce, lemon juice and chilli powder into a small saucepan and simmer over a medium-low heat for 3 minutes. Take the pan off the heat and thoroughly whisk in the oil.

★ Mix the carrots, peppers, onions, mushroom, courgettes, aubergine and garlic in a large bowl and coat with half of the dressing. Mix the lemon zest into the remaining dressing and set aside.

★ Tip the vegetables onto the preheated trays, arrange them to ensure they sit in a single layer on each tray and roast for 40 minutes, until cooked through.

★ Meanwhile, cook the lentils according to the packet instructions.

★ When the vegetables are roasted, squeeze the pulp from the 4 roasted garlic cloves out of the skins into the reserved dressing and whisk very well to combine. Add the dressing and lentils to the vegetables and mix well. Divide the mixture among 4 plates and crumble over the cheese. Grind over plenty of pepper and serve.

SIDE DISHES

SIDE DISHES

Roasted Butternut Squash

Squash comes into season during the autumn months, and this bourbon-spiked glaze works wonderfully with its natural sweetness to create a warming side dish. It's great with chicken, but also makes a perfect centrepiece for a vegetarian platter.

SERVES 4

1 large or 2 small butternut squash
8 garlic cloves, unpeeled
4 sprigs of rosemary

For the glaze
5 tablespoons Jim Beam® Bourbon
2 tablespoons olive oil
1 tablespoon clear honey
1 teaspoon dried chilli flakes
2 tablespoons butter
sea salt flakes and pepper

★ Preheat the oven to 160°C/180°C fan, Gas Mark 4.

★ Cut the squash lengthways into eight (if large) or quarters (if small). Remove and discard the seeds. Place the pieces of squash in a large roasting tin with the skin-sides facing down. Scatter the garlic and rosemary in among the squash.

★ To make the glaze, mix together the bourbon, olive oil, honey and chilli flakes with some sea salt and pepper in a small bowl. Drizzle this mixture over the squash, then dot with the butter. Roast for 30 minutes. Turn the squash, spoon over the juices and roast for a further 15–30 minutes or until tinged brown at the edges and softened all the way through. Serve immediately.

Charred Corn on the Cob with Whiskey Butter

Here, the trusty corn on the cob is given a super-charged bourbon butter drizzle –
a perfect unexpected twist for a barbecue side dish. Simply char the corn on the
barbecue or in a griddle pan, then drench it in the rich sauce – make sure you have
napkins at the ready!

SERVES 4

4 corn on the cob, husks removed

glug of rapeseed oil

For the whiskey butter

5 tablespoons Jim Beam® Bourbon

½ teaspoon chilli powder

2 teaspoons soy sauce

75g (2¾oz) unsalted butter

★ Prepare a barbecue to cook over medium-high heat, or set a griddle pan on the hob over a medium-high heat.

★ Coat the corn cobs with the oil and place them on the barbecue or in the griddle pan (or cook them in an open flame) until done to your liking, turning regularly.

★ To make the whiskey butter, put the bourbon into a small saucepan set over a medium heat and simmer for 3 minutes. Reduce the heat to low, stir in the chilli powder and soy sauce and melt in the butter.

★ When the corn is done, transfer it to a serving plate and drizzle over most of the bourbon butter – serve the remainder alongside the corn.

Baked Sweet Potatoes

Sweet potatoes are the ultimate no-fuss food – just sling them into the oven and let them do their thing. A spicy bourbon butter is a fantastic addition and takes no time at all to put together. Enjoy these as part of a picnic or barbecue, or they're great on their own for a simple weeknight dinner.

SERVES 4

4 sweet potatoes, skins pierced with a fork

For the bourbon butter

100ml (3½fl oz) Jim Beam® Bourbon

80g (2¾oz) slightly salted butter

1 heaped tablespoon finely chopped tarragon

2 small hot red chillies, deseeded and finely sliced

60g (2¼oz) Parmesan cheese, finely grated

pepper

★ Preheat the oven to 180°C/160°C fan, Gas Mark 4.

★ Place the sweet potatoes on a baking tray and bake for 45–60 minutes, until cooked through.

★ To make the bourbon butter, put the bourbon into a small saucepan and boil for 2 minutes. Meanwhile, put the butter into a shallow bowl. Once the whiskey has boiled for 2 minutes, pour it over the butter in the bowl and mash together with a fork. Stir in the remaining ingredients and set aside. (If you are making the bourbon butter in advance, roll it into a sausage shape using clingfilm, wrap it in the clingfilm and refrigerate until needed.)

★ Slice open the potatoes and fill each with a dollop of butter (or a slice of the butter, if made in advance and refrigerated).

Potato Wedges with Bourbon Barbecue Dip

Potato wedges make a great side dish to just about anything, and this super-intense barbecue dip, which takes less than ten minutes to prepare, helps to make them extra-special. The dip works brilliantly with normal fries as well, or with the chicken nuggets on page 40.

SERVES 4

For the bourbon barbecue dip

1 teaspoon smoked paprika

½ teaspoon garlic powder

2 tablespoons warm water

50ml (2fl oz) Jim Beam® Bourbon

2 tablespoons soy sauce

5 tablespoons ketchup

1 teaspoon treacle

For the potato wedges

800g (1lb 12oz) baking potatoes, cut into wedges

2 tablespoons rapeseed oil

pinch of sea salt flakes

★ Preheat the oven and a large nonstick baking tray to 200°C/180°C fan, Gas Mark 6.

★ To make the potato wedges, set a steamer basket over a pan of boiling water and steam the potato pieces for 5 minutes. Tip them onto a plate lined with kitchen paper and set aside for a couple of minutes, to allow the steam to evaporate, then pat them dry. Transfer them to a bowl, add the oil and toss to coat them in the oil. Now arrange the potato pieces on the preheated tray and bake for 30 minutes, until crispy on the outside and soft in the middle.

★ While the potatoes are baking, make the dip. Place the smoked paprika and garlic powder in a small bowl and mix with the measured warm water. Set aside. Heat the bourbon in a small saucepan over a medium-low heat and simmer for 2 minutes, then stir in the soy sauce, ketchup, treacle and the water, garlic and paprika mixture. Simmer for 5 minutes, stirring regularly, until the mixture has thickened and darkened. Transfer to a bowl and set aside to cool.

★ Sprinkle the potato wedges with salt flakes and serve with the dip.

Bourbon Boston Beans

Boston beans are the ultimate comfort food, but we've given them a Kentucky twist by adding a good slug of bourbon into the mix. The liquor adds a depth of flavour without overpowering the dish.

SERVES 4

1 tablespoon rapeseed oil

1 white onion, finely chopped

3 garlic cloves, crushed

150g (5½oz) pancetta, chopped, or smoked bacon lardons

2 cloves

pinch of sea salt

1 tablespoon tomato purée

2 x 400g (14oz) cans haricot beans, drained and rinsed

1 tablespoon Dijon mustard

1 teaspoon treacle

50ml (2fl oz) Jim Beam® Bourbon

150ml (¼ pint) good-quality chicken stock

★ Heat a large heavy-based saucepan with a lid over a high heat, then pour in the oil and heat it. Add the onion, garlic, bacon, cloves and salt and cook for 5 minutes, uncovered, until softened. Stir in the tomato purée and cook for 1 minute, then tip in the beans.

★ In a small jug, mix the mustard, treacle, bourbon and stock, then stir this into the beans in the saucepan. Bring the mixture to a simmer. Cover the saucepan with the lid, reduce the heat to low and cook for 30–40 minutes. Remove the cloves and serve immediately.

Bourbon and Chilli Cornbread

Spike a classic cornbread by making a hot mash with Jim Beam® Bourbon, with chilli flakes adding an extra kick. You'll need to start this dish a little while in advance to give the mash time to absorb. This cornbread makes a fantastic side dish for the Spiked Chilli Con Carne on page 70 or the Harvest Chilli on page 92.

SERVES 4

100ml (3½fl oz) Jim Beam® Bourbon

125g (4½oz) coarse polenta

100ml (3½fl oz) buttermilk

100g (3½oz) self-raising flour

pinch of salt

½ teaspoon bicarbonate of soda

½ tablespoon chilli flakes

1 large egg

½ tablespoon clear honey

50g (1¾oz) unsalted butter

★ Pour the bourbon into a small saucepan and bring to the boil. Meanwhile, put the polenta into a heatproof bowl. As soon as the bourbon comes to the boil, pour it over the polenta in the bowl and mix in the buttermilk. Set aside at room temperature for 3–6 hours.

★ Preheat the oven to 220°C/200°C fan, Gas Mark 7.

★ Mix the flour, salt, bicarbonate of soda and chilli flakes together in a bowl and set aside.

★ Using a balloon whisk, whisk the egg and honey into the soaked polenta, then add the dry ingredients and combine well.

★ Place the butter in a 20cm (8 inch) nonstick ovenproof frying pan set over a high heat. When the melted butter is very hot, take out 2 tablespoons and stir this into the batter. Pour the remainder into a small bowl and set aside.

★ Place the buttery pan back over a high heat, pour the batter into the pan and transfer the frying pan to the oven. Cook for 15 minutes, until golden and firm in the middle. Remove the frying pan from the oven, pour the remaining butter over the cornbread and serve immediately.

Everyday Bourbon Glaze

This spicy-sweet glaze offers a quick and easy way of bringing a huge hit of flavour to many a meal –
it works brilliantly with lamb chops, pork chops, duck, chicken (with skin on – if you want to
cook skinless poultry then try the bourbon and soy marinade on the opposite page), salmon,
white fish and vegetables. All you need to do is cook the food in the oven, on the hob or on
a barbecue as you normally would and, a few minutes before the end of the cooking time, remove
it from the heat source, spread over the glaze, then finish cooking as normal. Thick, sticky and
lightly spiced, it'll transform a plain meal into something really special.

SERVES 4+

2 tablespoons Jim Beam® Honey or
   Jim Beam® Bourbon
150g (5½oz) apricot jam
1½ tablespoons clear honey
½ tablespoon rapeseed oil
1 teaspoon dried chilli flakes
juice of ½ lime

★ Combine the ingredients in a small bowl and mix well. This glaze will keep
in a sealed container in the refrigerator for up to 2 weeks.

★ Once your meat, fish or vegetables are near to the end of cooking, brush
over some glaze and continue to cook for 5–10 minutes.

Simple Bourbon Marinade

Bourbon is a fantastic partner for soy sauce, and the combination makes an awesome quick-fix marinade that works with all sorts of meats and vegetables. Try it with red meat, skinless poultry, oily fish such as salmon, and hardy vegetables such as broccoli or portabello mushrooms. Best of all, there's no need to worry about marinating overnight, as the strong flavours need only 30 minutes to a couple of hours to work their magic.

SERVES 4

125ml (4fl oz) Jim Beam® Bourbon

2 shallots, finely chopped

2 tablespoons soy sauce

1½ tablespoons balsamic vinegar

½ tablespoon rapeseed oil

★ Put the bourbon and shallots into a small saucepan set over a medium-high heat, bring to the boil and simmer for 3 minutes, until the shallots have softened. Take the pan off the heat and stir in the remaining ingredients until well blended. Leave to cool completely. This marinade will keep in a sealed container in the refrigerator for up to 3 days.

★ Pat your meat or vegetables dry. Place them in a non-metallic bowl and mix with the marinade until well coated. Cover the bowl with clingfilm and refrigerate for a minimum of 30 minutes, turning the ingredients in the marinade occasionally. (If you prefer you can combine the ingredients with the marinade in a plastic food bag – ensure you squeeze out as much air as possible from the bag, and seal it well, before leaving it in the refrigerator for marinating.) Discard the marinade when ready to cook.

DESSERTS

DESSERTS

Bourbon Cherry Brownies

Everyone loves soft, gooey brownies, but in this recipe, we've stepped up the game even further by throwing bourbon-infused sour cherries into the mix. For an added whiskey kick, the brownies are drizzled with cherry-infused liquor once cooked to create the ultimate sticky chocolate treat.

MAKES 16

100ml (3½fl oz) Jim Beam® Bourbon

100g (3½oz) dried sour cherries

150g (5½oz) unsalted butter, cut into 4 pieces

150g (5½oz) dark chocolate (minimum 70 per cent cocoa solids), roughly broken up

2 large eggs

230g (8¼oz) caster sugar

75g (2¾oz) self-raising flour

2 tablespoons cocoa powder

pinch of salt

★ Put the bourbon and dried cherries into a small saucepan, bring to the boil and simmer for 3 minutes. Take the pan off the heat, cover with a lid and set aside until needed, to allow the cherries to absorb the bourbon.

★ Place the butter and chocolate pieces in a heatproof bowl set over a pan of gently simmering water and melt them together, stirring from time to time. Pour the mixture into a large mixing bowl and leave to cool a little.

★ Preheat the oven to 180°C/160°C fan, Gas Mark 4. Line a 20cm (8 inch) square baking tin with nonstick baking paper.

★ Put the eggs and sugar into a mixing bowl and beat with a hand-held electric beater for 3–5 minutes or until the mixture is smooth and glossy and almost meringue-like. Add this to the cooled chocolate and butter mixture and continue to beat until well combined. Fold in the flour, cocoa powder and salt.

★ Drain the cherries, reserving the liquor. Fold the cherries into the mixture.

★ Pour the mixture into the prepared tin, pushing it well into the corner. Smooth the top evenly using a rubber spatula or the back of a spoon.

★ Bake for 25–30 minutes, until the surface of the brownies begins to crack but there is still a wobble in the centre. Pierce the cake with a skewer and drizzle over the reserved liquor – this will dampen the surface, but it will soak in and make the brownies even better for it! For optimum flavour, set aside for a few hours to allow the cake to fully absorb the liquor, before cutting into 16 squares and serving.

Jim Beam® Pecan Pie

Give the classic pecan pie an extra kick with a little bourbon and maple syrup. The amount of filling here is exactly right for a 23cm (9 inch) flan tin; you need to be brave and fill it right to the top. Do this with the pie already on the baking sheet so the filling doesn't have as much opportunity to spill.

SERVES 8–10

250g (9oz) ready-made shortcrust pastry

150g (5½oz) pecan halves

vanilla ice cream and/or thick double cream, to serve

For the filling

80g (2¾oz) unsalted butter

200g (7oz) soft light brown sugar or light muscovado sugar

180g (6¼oz) maple syrup

½ teaspoon vanilla extract

100ml (3½fl oz) double cream

small pinch of salt

2 tablespoons cornflour

50ml (2fl oz) Jim Beam® Bourbon

2 large eggs, plus 1 large egg yolk

★ Roll out your pastry to a thickness of about 5mm (¼ inch). Use it to line a 23cm (9 inch) flan tin that is at least 3.5cm (1¼ inches) deep. Trim the pastry to fit the tin. Prick the base several times with a fork. Chill in the refrigerator for 30 minutes.

★ Preheat the oven to 200°C/180°C fan, Gas Mark 6. Line the pastry case with a sheet of nonstick baking paper and fill with baking beans or lentils. Bake for 15 minutes, then remove the baking paper and beans or lentils and bake for a further 5 minutes, until golden. Set aside to cool.

★ Spread the pecan halves on a baking sheet, transfer to the oven and toast for 5 minutes, until lightly toasted. Leave to cool. Reduce the oven temperature to 190°C/170°C fan, Gas Mark 5.

★ To make the filling, melt the butter in a heavy-based saucepan over a low heat. Remove the pan from the heat and gently whisk in the sugar, maple syrup, vanilla, double cream and salt. Return the pan to the heat and stir for 2–3 minutes, until the sugar has dissolved.

★ In a small cup, mix the cornflour with about 1 tablespoon of the bourbon to form a smooth paste. Take the saucepan off the heat and whisk in the cornflour paste. Return the pan to the heat and whisk gently for 5 minutes, until the mixture has thickened slightly, to the consistency of double cream, and is smooth and glossy. Set aside to cool for 15 minutes, then whisk in the eggs, one at a time, followed by the egg yolk. Stir in the remaining bourbon and transfer the filling to a jug.

★ Sit the pastry-lined flan tin on a baking sheet and scatter the pecan halves into the pastry case. Pull the centre rack part way out of the oven and place the baking sheet on it. Carefully pour the filling into the pastry case, over the pecans. Fill it as much as possible, ideally so that the filling is level with the top of the pastry. Bake for 35–40 minutes, until just set. Remove from the oven, set the tin on a wire rack and leave to cool completely. Serve with vanilla ice cream and/or double cream.

DESSERTS

Kentucky Carrot Cake

Here's a recipe for a decadent fruity carrot cake, with bourbon in both the batter and the icing.
You have to go all-in and use full-fat cream cheese here – low-fat won't work. This delicious cake
will be eaten in no time, but if you do have any leftovers, keep them refrigerated so the icing
stays fresh. The icing quantity here gives enough to fill and top the cake. If you want to cover
the sides as well, increase the quantities by half again.

SERVES 8–10

For the cake

100ml (3½fl oz) Jim Beam® Bourbon

100g (3½oz) sultanas

225g (8oz) self-raising flour

1 teaspoon baking powder

1 teaspoon ground cinnamon

small pinch of salt

200g (7oz) dark brown muscovado sugar

250g (9oz) carrots, coarsely grated

75g (2¾oz) pecan nuts, roughly chopped

finely grated zest of 1 large orange

150ml (¼ pint) sunflower oil

3 eggs, lightly beaten

For the icing

100g (3½oz) unsalted butter, softened

150g (5½oz) icing sugar

3 tablespoons Jim Beam® Bourbon

200g (7oz) full-fat cream cheese

reserved orange zest (see method)

25g (1oz) pecan nuts, to decorate

★ To make the cake, pour the bourbon into a small saucepan and add the sultanas. Heat gently, without allowing the liquid to come to the boil, for 5 minutes. Set aside to cool.

★ Preheat the oven to 200°C/180°C fan/Gas Mark 6. Line the bases of 2 x 20-cm (8-inch) round cake tins with nonstick baking paper.

★ Sift the flour, baking powder and cinnamon into a large mixing bowl. Mix in the salt, sugar, carrots, nuts and roughly two-thirds of the orange zest (reserve the rest for the icing). Add the oil, eggs and soaked sultanas, along with any bourbon left in the pan, and mix thoroughly.

★ Divide the mixture equally between the prepared cake tins and gently smooth the surfaces. Bake for 25–30 minutes, until risen and a skewer inserted in the centre of each cake comes out clean. Leave to cool in the tins for 5 minutes, then turn out the cakes onto a wire rack and leave to cool completely.

★ For the icing, put the butter and icing sugar into a mixing bowl and use a hand-held electric beater to beat them together until smooth. Now gradually whisk in the bourbon. Add the cream cheese and reserved orange zest and whisk until smooth.

★ When the cakes are completely cold, place one cake layer on a cake board or serving plate and top with half the icing. Level out the icing until it is spread evenly across the surface of the cake. Align the second cake layer on top, then top with the remaining icing, again, smoothing it out to an even thickness. Chop the pecan nuts and scatter over the cake to finish.

DESSERTS

Fruit Cake Loaf

This easy fruit cake recipe is great for making a mid-morning treat, but you will need to soak the raisins in Jim Beam® Honey (or use Jim Beam® Bourbon, if you prefer) the day before you intend to bake. This cake is best served the day after baking (it only gets better as time goes on!).

MAKES 12 SLICES

450g (1lb) mixed dried fruit, such as vine fruits, cherries, cranberries, chopped mixed peel, chopped dates, chopped figs or chopped apricots

150ml (¼ pint) Jim Beam® Honey

80g (2¾oz) unsalted butter

75g (2¾oz) soft brown sugar

55g (2oz) apricot jam

2 small eggs

65g (2¼oz) pecan nuts, broken into small pieces

80g (2¾oz) plain flour, sifted

½ teaspoon baking powder

★ Place the mixed fruit in a large, shallow bowl and cover with 100ml (3½fl oz) of the bourbon. Leave to soak for 24 hours, mixing occasionally. When preparing to bake, drain the dried fruits and discard the liquor.

★ Preheat the oven to 160°C/140°C fan, Gas Mark 3. Select a 900g (2lb) loaf tin and line it with 2 layers of nonstick baking paper to prevent the loaf from sticking.

★ Cream together the butter, sugar and jam, beating well until the mixture becomes paler, then add the eggs and beat for a further 3 minutes. Using a spoon, fold in the drained fruit and the nuts.

★ In a separate bowl, combine the flour and baking powder, then gently fold into the cake mixture.

★ Pour the mixture into the prepared loaf tin and bake for 1 hour. Reduce the oven temperature to 130°C/110°C fan, Gas Mark ¾. Cover the top of the loaf tin tightly with a double layer of kitchen foil, then bake for a further 30 minutes or until a skewer inserted into the centre of the cake comes out clean.

★ Pierce the cake all over with a skewer. Over the course of the next hour, drizzle the remaining bourbon into the holes with a small spoon. Leave the cake to cool completely in the tin.

★ The cake is best served the day after baking, and gets better as time goes on. If there is any left over, it will keep for at least a week, wrapped in kitchen foil and stored in an airtight tin.

Apple Crumble with Beam-infused Cream

Apple partners beautifully with bourbon so, for this delicious dish, we've trebled up by adding Jim Beam® Bourbon to the apple filling, the crumble topping and the vanilla cream to spoon over! If you prefer, make this with Jim Beam® Honey instead, for a slightly sweeter taste.

SERVES 4–6

For the topping

50g (1¾oz) pecan nuts

25g (1oz) porridge oats

125g (4½oz) plain flour

1 teaspoon ground cinnamon

small pinch of salt

100g (3½oz) unsalted butter, diced

100g (3½oz) demerara sugar, plus 2 tablespoons for sprinkling

2 tablespoons Jim Beam® Bourbon or Jim Beam® Honey

For the filling

800g (1lb 12oz) peeled, cored cooking apples (such as Bramley)

50–100g (1¾–3½oz) golden caster sugar (according to the sweetness of the apples)

125ml (4fl oz) Jim Beam® Bourbon or Jim Beam® Honey

5 tablespoons maple syrup

For the bourbon cream

450ml (16fl oz) double cream

3 tablespoons Jim Beam® Bourbon or Jim Beam® Honey

1 tablespoon golden caster sugar

1 teaspoon vanilla extract

★ Preheat the oven to 190°C/170°C fan, Gas Mark 5. Select a baking dish measuring roughly 20 x 30cm (8 x 12 inches) that is at least 4cm (1½ inches) deep.

★ To make the topping, tip the nuts and oats into a food processor and blitz until coarsely ground. Add the remaining topping ingredients, except the 2 tablespoons demerara sugar and bourbon, and pulse until the mixture has the consistency of coarse breadcrumbs. Set aside.

Recipe continues overleaf ➤⟶

* For the filling, chop the apples into rough chunks until you have 800g (1lb 12oz). Tip them into a saucepan with 50g (1¾oz) of the caster sugar and the bourbon, cover and cook over a medium heat for 5–10 minutes, until the apples collapse. Stir in the maple syrup, taste and add more sugar if needed. Spoon the mixture into the baking dish. If there is a lot of liquid, use a slotted spoon to transfer the apples, then boil the liquid for 2–3 minutes until it has reduced to a syrupy consistency, and add this to the baking dish.

* Tip the crumble mixture into the baking dish to cover the fruit loosely. Sprinkle the topping with the remaining demerara sugar and the bourbon. Place the dish on a baking tray and bake for 40 minutes, until the topping is golden-brown and the apples are bubbling at the edges.

* To make the bourbon cream, lightly whip the double cream to very soft peaks, then whisk in the remaining ingredients.

* Serve the crumble hot or warm with the bourbon cream on the side.

Jim Beam® Cherry Pie

As if lacing a rich cherry pie with bourbon wasn't special enough, this dish also has a secret layer of marzipan at the base – it doesn't get much better than that! Cook it in a metal pie dish to ensure your pastry is beautifully crisp, and serve the pie with a spoonful of vanilla ice cream on the side. Illustrated overleaf.

SERVES 4–6

650g (1lb 7oz) canned black cherries, drained and halved

175g (6oz) black cherry conserve

1½ tablespoons lemon juice

3 tablespoons Jim Beam® Bourbon

500g (1lb 2oz) ready-made shortcrust pastry

200g (7oz) marzipan

splash of milk

½ tablespoon demerara sugar

vanilla ice cream, to serve

★ Place the cherries, conserve and lemon juice in a large saucepan, bring to a fast simmer and simmer, uncovered, for 20–25 minutes or until thick and not much liquid remains. Take the pan off the heat, stir in the bourbon and leave to cool completely.

★ Select a 23-cm (9-inch) pie tin with a capacity of 700ml (1¼ pints). Roll out two-thirds of the pastry to about 5mm (¼ inch). Cover the remaining pastry with clingfilm and set aside in the refrigerator. Use the pastry circle to line the base of the pie tin, leaving the excess pastry overhanging the edges of the tin. Roll out the marzipan to a circle roughly 2.5cm (1 inch) wider than the base of the tin. Lay this over the pastry at the bottom of the tin and just up the sides. Cover the tin with clingfilm and chill in the refrigerator until ready to use.

★ Preheat the oven to 200°C/180°C fan, Gas Mark 6.

★ Tip the cold cherry mixture into the pie tin over the layer of marzipan. Roll out the remaining pastry to the same thickness as the pastry base. Brush the edges of the pastry in the tin with a little milk, then lay the pastry circle over the top and press down firmly around the edges of the tin with a fork to seal the lid to the base firmly. Trim away excess pastry with scissors, cutting a little away from the rim of the tin to allow for shrinkage. Brush the top of the pie with milk, then make 4 small slits in the centre of the pie to allow steam to escape during baking. Sprinkle over the sugar.

★ Place the tin on a baking tray and bake for 30–40 minutes. Leave to cool in the tin a little, then serve warm with ice cream.

Bourbon Pear Tarte Tatin

This impressive-looking dessert uses a somewhat easier method than a classic tarte tatin, which is traditionally cooked in one pan. If you have time, soak the pears in bourbon overnight, but if you're in a hurry, you can skip this step and it'll still taste great. Be careful when you invert the cooked tarte, as some hot juices may spill out. Serve this dish with a simple vanilla ice cream.

SERVES 4

400g (14oz) or 3–4 unripe hard pears (such as Conference pears), peeled, cored and quartered lengthways

50–75ml (2–2½fl oz) Jim Beam® Honey or Jim Beam® Bourbon

2 tablespoons light brown sugar

2 tablespoons caster sugar

20g (¾oz) unsalted butter

pinch of salt

plain flour, for dusting

200g (7oz) ready-rolled all-butter puff pastry

vanilla ice cream, to serve

★ Submerge the pears in the bourbon in a shallow bowl. Cover with clingfilm and refrigerate overnight. The next day, remove the pears, reserve the liquor and pat the pears dry using kitchen paper.

★ Preheat the oven to 180°C/160°C fan, Gas Mark 4.

★ Place both types of sugar in a small saucepan with 1 tablespoon of the reserved liquor. Set the pan over a medium-high heat and boil for 3–5 minutes or until the mixture becomes darker in colour. Add the butter and, once melted, add the pears and salt. Cook for about 2 minutes, until the pears are warmed through and coated in the mixture.

★ Lightly dust your work surface with flour, then roll out the pastry so that it is about 5mm (¼ inch) thick. Select a 23-cm (9-inch) pie tin with a capacity of 700ml (1¼ pints). Invert the tin over the pastry and use the rim of the tin as a guide to cut out a circle of pastry, working 1cm (½ inch) away from the rim.

★ Arrange the pears, with the skin-sides facing down, in the pie tin. Pour over most of the remaining reserved liquor, reserving 2 tablespoons for serving. Lay the circle of pastry over the pears and tuck the edges into the tin around the pears.

★ Place the tin on a baking tray and bake for 45 minutes. Leave to cool in the tin for 5 minutes, than place a serving plate over the top and carefully invert the plate and tin to transfer the tarte to the plate. Leave to rest for 5 minutes, then serve warm with ice cream, and drizzle ½ tablespoon of the reserved liquor over each serving.

Rhubarb and Ginger Upside-down Cake

An awesome combination of sweet buttery syrup, tart rhubarb, warm ginger and a gentle kick of bourbon, this cake is a real treat. For added crunch, you can top it with sugar, then caramelize it with a cook's blowtorch, but it's delicious even without this. Any stone fruit, such as plums, would work well in place of rhubarb, and you can replace the Jim Beam® Bourbon with Jim Beam® Honey, if you prefer.

SERVES 8

thick Greek-style full-fat
   unsweetened yogurt, to serve

For the rhubarb syrup

50g (1¾oz) unsalted butter

100g (3½oz) caster sugar

50ml (2fl oz) ginger syrup from a jar
   of stem ginger

50ml (2fl oz) Jim Beam® Bourbon

400g (14oz) rhubarb, cut into 10-cm
   (4-inch) lengths

For the cake

200g (7oz) unsalted butter, at room
   temperature

200g (7oz) caster sugar

3 large eggs

50g (1¾oz) stem ginger, grated

50g (1¾oz) ground almonds

pinch of salt

200g (7oz) self-raising flour

15ml–50ml (½–2fl oz) milk

granulated sugar (optional)

★ To make the rhubarb syrup, put the butter, sugar and ginger syrup into a large saucepan and bring to the boil. Stir in the bourbon and rhubarb and, once the mixture returns to the boil, take the pan off the heat and set aside.

★ Preheat the oven to 180°C/160°C fan, Gas Mark 4. Take a large sheet of nonstick baking paper, scrunch it up, then flatten it out again and use it to roughly line a 20cm (8 inch) cake tin, allowing plenty of paper to overhang the edges of the tin.

★ To make the cake, put the butter and sugar into a large bowl and beat with a hand-held electric beater for 3 minutes, until pale and fluffy. Now add the eggs one at a time, beating each egg into the mixture thoroughly before adding the next. Using a large spoon, stir in the stem ginger, ground almonds and salt.

★ Sift in the flour and combine with minimal stirring, then stir in 1 tablespoon of the milk at a time, adding just enough get the mixture to the point where it drops off the spoon easily.

★ Remove the rhubarb from the syrup using a slotted spoon and arrange it across the bottom of the cake tin. Pour over 120ml (4fl oz) of the syrup, reserving the rest. Spoon the cake batter carefully over the rhubarb and syrup, pushing it into the corners without disturbing the syrup.

★ Bake for 45 minutes. The cake is cooked when a skewer inserted in the centre comes out clean. Using a skewer, pierce holes into the sponge and drizzle over the reserved syrup. Leave to rest for 15 minutes.

★ Cover the tin with a serving plate and invert the plate and tin so the cake rests on the plate. Carefully remove the baking paper. If liked, sprinkle the rhubarb generously with the granulated sugar and caramelize the sugar using a cook's blowtorch. Serve with thick Greek yogurt.

Whiskey Baked Apples with Yogurt

As simple as a great dessert gets, this one can be thrown together at the last minute – just pop it in the oven when you're eating your main course and it'll be ready by the time you're ready for it. Of course, Jim Beam® Apple is a good choice for this dish, but either Jim Beam® Bourbon or Jim Beam® Honey work well too. Whichever style of bourbon you choose, it will give you a delicious cooking liquor to drizzle over the baked apples when you serve.

SERVES 4

4 cooking apples

80ml (2¾fl oz) Jim Beam® Apple

60g (2¼oz) mixed dried fruit (such as vine fruits, cherries or cranberries)

60g (2¼oz) nuts (such as walnuts, pecans or almonds), broken into small pieces

2–4 tablespoons demerara sugar

30g (1oz) unsalted butter, cut into small cubes

clear honey, to taste

50ml (2fl oz) water

250ml (9fl oz) thick Greek-style full-fat unsweetened yogurt

★ Preheat the oven to 200°C/180°C fan, Gas Mark 6.

★ Score the skin of each apple around the widest part. Core the apples, then place them in an ovenproof dish, ensuring they fit snugly.

★ Mix 50ml (2fl oz) of the bourbon with the mixed fruit, nuts and sugar in a medium bowl.

★ Push a cube of butter into the central cavity of each apple, then fill the hole with the fruit-and-nut mixture. Tip the remaining mixture around the apples, then drizzle over a little honey. Cover the dish with kitchen foil.

★ Bake for 45 minutes, then remove the foil and stir in the measured water. Bake, uncovered, for a further 15 minutes, until the apple flesh begins to expand underneath the skin.

★ Stir the remaining bourbon into the yogurt and sweeten the mixture with honey to taste.

★ Serve each apple with some of the syrupy sauce from the dish and the sweetened bourbon yogurt.

New York Bourbon Cheesecake

This creamy, indulgent cheesecake keeps well in the refrigerator for a couple of days, so is great
for entertaining, as you can make it in advance and top it with berries just before you serve.
If you don't have a food processor, put the biscuits in a freezer bag and bash them with
a rolling pin to make the crumbs for the base.

SERVES 10–12

For the base

**250g (9oz) chocolate digestive
biscuits**

**100g (3½oz) unsalted butter, melted,
plus 1 tablespoon for greasing**

3 tablespoons demerara sugar

For the topping

**600g (1lb 5oz) full-fat cream cheese,
at room temperature if possible**

250g (9oz) golden caster sugar

50ml (2fl oz) Jim Beam® Bourbon

1 tablespoon plain flour

1 teaspoon vanilla extract

small pinch of salt

2 large eggs

400ml (14fl oz) soured cream

fresh berries, to serve

★ Preheat the oven to 200°C/180°C fan, Gas Mark 6.

★ Select a 20-cm (8-inch) loose-bottomed tart tin with a depth of about
7cm (2¾ inches). Line the base with nonstick baking paper and brush
the sides with melted butter.

★ To make the base, blitz the biscuits in a food processor until they take on
the consistency of coarse crumbs. Add the melted butter and blitz again.
Finally, add the demerara sugar and blitz once to just combine. Press the
mixture into the tin, packing it in firmly. Level it out to an even thickness
using the back of a spoon.

★ For the topping, beat the cream cheese with a wooden spoon until it is smooth
(alternatively, use a stand mixer fitted with a paddle attachment). Mix in the sugar,
bourbon, flour, vanilla and salt. Beat in the eggs one at a time, followed by 150ml
(¼ pint) of the soured cream. If at any point the mixture looks lumpy, switch to
using a sturdy balloon whisk. Pour the mixture over the cheesecake base.

★ Sit the tin on a baking sheet and bake for 10 minutes. Reduce the oven
temperature to 170°C/150°C fan, Gas Mark 3½ and bake for a further
30 minutes, or until the cheesecake is partially set but still has a wobble in
the middle. Turn off the oven and leave the cheesecake in the oven with the
door shut for 1 hour to set.

★ Remove the cheesecake from the oven and leave to cool completely at room
temperature. Pour the remaining soured cream over the cheesecake and
spread it to cover the surface completely. Transfer the tin to the refrigerator
and chill overnight. To serve, remove the cheesecake from the tin, cut it into
slices and serve chilled, topped with berries.

Whiskey and Dark Chocolate Mousse Cake

Chocolate and bourbon – flavour combinations don't get much more appealing than that. This rich, intense mousse cake is the perfect example. Serve it chilled, with double cream. For added decadence, include Jim Beam® Double Oak Bourbon in the topping, but Jim Beam® Bourbon will work just as well. For a slightly less potent version, omit the bourbon from the topping, or reduce it to just 1 teaspoon. Illustrated overleaf.

SERVES 8–10

For the mousse cake

150g (5½oz) good-quality dark chocolate, broken into pieces

150g (5½oz) unsalted butter, diced

150g (5½oz) golden caster sugar

2 tablespoons double cream

1 teaspoon vanilla extract

3 eggs

5 tablespoons Jim Beam® Bourbon

For the topping

150g (5½oz) good-quality dark chocolate, very finely chopped

150ml (¼ pint) double cream

4 teaspoons Jim Beam® Bourbon or Jim Beam® Double Oak Bourbon

pinch of sea salt flakes, plus extra to serve (optional)

double cream, to serve

★ Preheat the oven to 180°C/160°C fan, Gas Mark 4. Line the base and sides of a 20-cm (8-inch) round cake tin with nonstick baking paper.

★ To make the mousse cake, put all the ingredients, except the eggs and bourbon, into a large, heavy-based saucepan. Stir gently over a low heat until the chocolate and butter have almost melted, then take the pan off the heat and stir gently until the mixture is completely smooth. Leave to cool for 5 minutes, then use a balloon whisk to beat in the eggs one at a time. Beat in the bourbon until the mixture is smooth and glossy.

★ Pour the batter into the prepared tin, sit the tin on a baking sheet and bake for 45 minutes, until just set but still a little soft in the middle. Leave in the tin to cool completely.

★ For the topping, put the chocolate into a large heatproof bowl. In a saucepan, gently bring the cream to a simmer over a medium heat, ensuring you do not let it come to the boil, then remove the pan from the heat and pour the hot cream over the chocolate. Leave for 30 seconds (the heat from the cream will gradually melt the chocolate), then use a balloon whisk to mix the cream and chocolate together quickly. As soon as they come together into a smooth, shiny mixture, gradually stir in the bourbon and salt.

★ Place a serving plate over the cake tin and invert the plate and tin together to transfer the cooled cake onto the plate. Carefully remove the baking paper (don't worry if the surface of the cake breaks up a little – the topping will cover this). Pour over the warm topping and spread it across the top and sides to coat the cake. Leave to cool completely, then chill in the refrigerator for at least 3 hours, or for up to 3 days.

★ Sprinkle with a little extra sea salt just before serving, if you like. Serve in thin slices with softly whipped double cream.

Bourbon Chocolate Truffles

These truffles are mind-blowing and (if you can bear to part with them) make perfect gifts. Before rolling, you can keep the mixture in the refrigerator for up to 5 days, or in the freezer for up to a month (just defrost at room temperature for about 2 hours before rolling). Just one word of warning – it's absolutely crucial that you don't allow the cream to boil when making the truffle mixture, or the chocolate can become grainy. For a stronger bourbon flavour, use Jim Beam® Double Oak Bourbon.

MAKES ABOUT 30

For the chocolate truffles

200g (7oz) good-quality dark chocolate, finely chopped

200ml double cream

15g (½oz) unsalted butter

25ml (1fl oz) Jim Beam® Bourbon or Jim Beam® Double Oak Bourbon

small pinch of sea salt

To decorate

4 tablespoons cocoa powder

75g (2¾oz) finely chopped pecan nuts, toasted

100g (3½oz) dark and/or milk chocolate, melted

★ To make the truffles, put the chocolate into a heatproof bowl. In a saucepan, gently bring the cream and butter to a simmer over a medium heat, ensuring you do not allow the mixture to come to the boil, then remove the pan from the heat and pour the mixture over the chocolate in the bowl. Leave for 30 seconds (the heat from the cream will gradually melt the chocolate), then mix using a balloon whisk. As soon as everything has come together into a smooth, shiny mixture, gradually stir in the bourbon and mix in the salt. Set aside to cool, then cover and chill for at least 4 hours until firm (or you can freeze it at this stage).

★ To roll the truffles, remove the mixture from the refrigerator 10 minutes before starting.

★ Roll teaspoonfuls of the mixture quickly between your palms (if you have hot palms, roll using your fingertips). Place the rolled truffles on a tray lined with nonstick baking paper.

★ To decorate, put the cocoa powder into one shallow bowl, and the chopped nuts into another. Roll one-third of the truffles in cocoa powder and one-third in the chopped nuts. Coat the remaining truffles in the melted chocolate: dip them in the melted chocolate, use 2 forks to roll them in the liquid and to lift them out, then transfer them to a tray lined with nonstick baking paper and leave to cool. (Once cool, you can drizzle over a contrasting melted chocolate, if you like.) Keep the truffles refrigerated until ready to serve.

Easy Chocolate, Bourbon and Raisin Ice Cream

The beauty of this recipe is that you don't need an ice cream maker, or to spend hours hand-churning, as the addition of Jim Beam® Bourbon keeps the ice cream silky smooth and scoopable. And it tastes incredible to boot! Remove it from the freezer a few minutes before serving to allow it to loosen up a little.

SERVES 4–8

For the Jim Beam® raisins
150ml (¼ pint) Jim Beam® Bourbon
150g (5½oz) raisins
3 tablespoons golden caster sugar

For the ice cream base
4 egg yolks
150g (5½oz) golden caster sugar
100g (3½oz) dark chocolate, roughly chopped
1½ tablespoons unsweetened cocoa powder
400ml (14fl oz) double cream
100ml (3½fl oz) milk
1 teaspoon vanilla extract
¼ teaspoon sea salt flakes
50ml (2fl oz) Jim Beam® Bourbon

★ For the Jim Beam® raisins, pour the bourbon into a small saucepan and add the raisins and sugar. Bring to a simmer, then simmer gently over a medium heat for 5 minutes. Set aside to cool. When cool, remove the raisins with a slotted spoon, then return them to any residual bourbon in the pan.

★ Put the egg yolks and 50g (1¾oz) of the caster sugar into a large heatproof mixing bowl and, using a hand-held electric beater, whisk until the mixture is thick and pale.

★ Put the chocolate and cocoa into a separate large heatproof bowl.

★ Pour the cream, milk and remaining caster sugar into a large heavy-based saucepan. Stir over a medium heat until the sugar has dissolved and the mixture reaches a simmer, but don't let it come to the boil. Remove the pan from the heat and leave to stand for 30 seconds, then pour the mixture over the chocolate and cocoa. Whisk quickly with a balloon whisk until the chocolate has melted.

★ Very slowly add ladlefuls of the chocolate mixture to the egg yolks and sugar mixture, whisking continuously with the electric beaters, until half the chocolate mixture is mixed in, after which you can pour it in more quickly. Whisk in the vanilla and salt.

★ Return the mixture to the saucepan, set it over a low heat and stir it continuously for 10 minutes, or until steaming hot and thickened to the consistency of double cream. Pour the mixture through a sieve into a freezer-safe bowl, stir in the bourbon, plus the raisins and their soaking liquor and leave to cool. Once cool, freeze overnight, or for up to 2 weeks, before serving.

Kentucky Bourbon Chocolate Shake

This is the Jim Beam® take on an American diner classic – the chocolate milkshake. This recipe can be chopped and changed to suit your mood. Reduce the ice cream by 100g (3½oz) and increase the ice quantity for a thinner, less rich version, or add a splash more bourbon if you want an added kick. Pop a couple of freezer-safe glasses into the freezer to chill before serving to keep things extra cool on a hot day.

MAKES 4 SHAKES

500g (1lb 2oz) good-quality vanilla ice cream

8 tablespoons chocolate-hazelnut spread (such as Nutella)

120ml (4fl oz) milk

80ml (2¾fl oz) Jim Beam® Honey or Jim Beam® Bourbon

120g (4¼oz) ice cubes or crushed ice

★ Put all the ingredients into a blender and blend to a thick, smooth, icy consistency. Pour into glasses, add straws and a spoon and drink straight away while cold and thick.

CLASSIC COCKTAILS

CLASSIC COCKTAILS

Happy Hollow Hedgerow

Nestled in the rolling foothills of Kentucky, Happy Hollow is the home of the Jim Beam American Stillhouse. This fruity summer cocktail perfectly encapsulates the feeling of the long summer evenings there. If you can't find sparkling elderflower, try using old-fashioned cloudy lemonade instead.

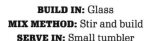

BUILD IN: Glass
MIX METHOD: Stir and build
SERVE IN: Small tumbler

1 part Jim Beam® Apple

1 scant part Chambord® Liqueur

3 parts sparkling elderflower, or
  to top up

2–3 fresh blackberries per drink,
  to garnish

★ Pour the Jim Beam® Apple and Chambord® Liqueur into a tumbler filled with a handful of crushed ice. Stir well and top up with the sparkling elderflower. Garnish with the blackberries and serve.

Jim's Mint Julep

A close relative of the mojito, the mint julep provides a classic way to enjoy a bourbon cocktail on a hot summer's day. It keeps things simple – just bourbon, sweetened with sugar syrup, topped up with soda water and laced with fresh mint leaves – and is all the better for it.

BUILD IN: Glass
MIX METHOD: Stir and build
SERVE IN: Tumbler

handful of mint leaves per drink

2 parts Jim Beam Black® Bourbon or
Jim Beam® Double Oak Bourbon

½ part sugar syrup

soda water, to top up

★ Fill a tumbler with crushed ice. Screw up the mint leaves in your palm (to release the oils), then drop them into the glass. Add the bourbon and sugar syrup and stir to mix. Top up with soda water and serve.

Apple and Maple Mule

This cocktail pairs Jim Beam® Apple with ginger ale, cut through with a dash of lime juice and balanced with the sweetness of maple syrup, to make a refreshing long drink for handing out at get-togethers. Think of this drink as a supercharged bourbon take on the classic Moscow Mule cocktail.

BUILD IN: Highball glass
MIX METHOD: Stir and build
SERVE IN: Highball glass

2 parts Jim Beam® Apple

½ part maple syrup

½ part freshly squeezed lime juice

8 parts ginger ale, or to top up

To garnish

slice of green apple or lime per drink

1 sprig of mint per drink

★ Pour the bourbon, maple syrup and lime juice into a highball glass and stir well until the maple syrup has dissolved. Add a handful of ice cubes and top up with ginger ale. Garnish with a slice of apple or lime and a sprig of mint, then serve.

Honey Beam Blush

Think of this light and fruity cocktail as a Jim Beam® take on the classic Cosmopolitan.
It's a perfect drink for a summer gathering. To really make the most of this combination,
be sure to squeeze a fresh orange rather than using juice out of a carton. It's most definitely
worth the extra effort.

BUILD IN: Shaker
MIX METHOD: Shake and strain
SERVE IN: Martini glass

1 part Jim Beam® Honey

2 parts cranberry juice

½ part freshly squeezed orange juice

strip of pared orange peel cut to a
width of 1cm (½ inch) per drink, to
garnish

★ Pour the bourbon, cranberry juice and orange juice into a cocktail shaker.
Add 2–3 ice cubes and shake. Strain the mixture into a small martini glass.
Twist the strip of orange peel over the glass to release the oil into the cocktail,
then drop it into the drink as a garnish and serve.

Sour Jim

A whiskey sour is a wonderful thing! And this is the ultimate recipe for one, allowing you to enjoy the unique flavours of Jim Beam®. Perfectly balanced, blending creaminess with sharp lemon juice, this drink is at its best when made with Jim Beam Black® Bourbon or Jim Beam® Double Oak Bourbon, but it's still delicious with Jim Beam® Bourbon.

BUILD IN: Shaker
MIX METHOD: Shake and strain
SERVE IN: Tumbler

2 parts Jim Beam Black® Bourbon or Jim Beam® Double Oak Bourbon

1 part egg white

1 scant part freshly squeezed lemon juice

1 scant part sugar syrup

2–3 drops Angostura® bitters per drink, to garnish

★ Pour the bourbon, egg white, lemon juice and sugar syrup into a cocktail shaker. Add 2–3 ice cubes and shake vigorously for 30 seconds. Strain the mixture into a tumbler filled with ice cubes, garnish with Angostura® bitters and serve.

Clermont Champagne

A simple, light and refreshing way to enjoy bourbon, this is the perfect drink for serving at a special event or celebration. Illustrated overleaf.

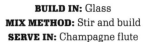

BUILD IN: Glass
MIX METHOD: Stir and build
SERVE IN: Champagne flute

1 brown sugar cube per drink

2 dashes of Angostura® bitters
  per drink

1 part Jim Beam® Bourbon

4–5 parts sparkling wine

★ Place the sugar cube into a champagne flute. Shake the Angostura® bitters onto the sugar cube. Pour in the bourbon and slowly top up with sparkling wine, then serve.

Bardstown Boulevardier

A cousin of the Negroni, this drink is named in honour of Bardstown, near the
Jim Beam American Stillhouse, in the heart of Kentucky. Balancing bitter and
sweet, it's a rich, warming cocktail that's best garnished with a twist
of fresh orange. Illustrated overleaf.

BUILD IN: Glass
MIX METHOD: Stir and build
SERVE IN: Tumbler

1 part Jim Beam® Black Bourbon or
  Jim Beam® Double Oak Bourbon

½ part Aperol® Aperitivo or
  Campari® Liqueur

½ part sweet (red) vermouth

strip of pared orange peel cut to
  a width of 1cm (½ inch) per drink,
  to garnish

★ Half-fill a tumbler with ice cubes. Add the bourbon, Aperol® Aperitivo
or Campari® Liqueur and vermouth and stir gently to combine. Garnish
with a twist of orange zest and serve.

Cherry Picker

This is a supercharged throwback to a 1950s classic – the cola float –
but with a kick. Sweet, cool, fizzy and fun, you'll need a straw and a long
spoon to serve it up with.

BUILD IN: Glass
MIX METHOD: Stir and build
SERVE IN: Short-stemmed wine glass

1–2 scoops vanilla ice cream
  per drink

2 parts Jim Beam® Bourbon

8–10 parts cherry cola

1 maraschino cherry per drink, to
  garnish

★ Place a scoop of vanilla ice cream into a short-stemmed wine glass. Pour in
the bourbon, then slowly top up with cherry cola. Stir gently – it will fizz up a
little. Top with a second scoop of ice cream, if you like, garnish with a cherry
and serve with a straw and a long spoon.

Long Lick Lemonade

Long Lick Creek runs past the Jim Beam distillery, and this homage to old-fashioned lemonade is the kind of drink that we enjoy there on lazy summer afternoons. Fizzy, zesty and delicious, it's one to sip as you watch the sun go down.

BUILD IN: Glass
MIX METHOD: Stir and build
SERVE IN: Highball or tumbler

1 part Jim Beam® Bourbon

1 part sugar syrup

½ part freshly squeezed lemon juice

thin strip of pared orange peel
  per drink

tonic or soda water, to taste

★ Fill a highball glass or tumbler with a handful of ice cubes. Add the bourbon, sugar syrup, lemon juice and orange peel. Stir gently to combine, top up with tonic or soda water and serve.

Jim Beam® Maple Fizz

Maple, with its sweet, woody flavour, goes very well with bourbon, and this fizzy cocktail makes the very most of that happy marriage. Like the Sour Jim (see page 162), it's made with egg white to add creaminess, and spiked with sharp lemon juice to balance the flavours, for an intriguing and refreshing drink.

BUILD IN: Shaker
MIX METHOD: Shake and build
SERVE IN: Highball glass

1½ parts Jim Beam® Bourbon

scant part maple syrup

½ part freshly squeezed lemon juice

a dash of double cream per drink

1 part egg white

3 parts soda water, or to top up

1 whole star anise or slice of lemon per drink, to garnish (optional)

★ Pour the bourbon, maple syrup, lemon juice, double cream and egg white into a cocktail shaker. Add 2–3 ice cubes and shake vigorously for 30 seconds.

★ Fill a highball glass with ice cubes. Strain the mixture over the ice and top up with soda water. Garnish the cocktail with a star anise or lemon slice, if you like, and serve.

Kentucky Manhattan

Warm, smoky and bitter, this cocktail brings to mind the classic Manhattan.
It's a sophisticated drink that beautifully balances the vanilla notes of bourbon
with aromatic vermouth.

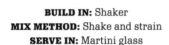

BUILD IN: Shaker
MIX METHOD: Shake and strain
SERVE IN: Martini glass

2 parts Jim Beam Black® Bourbon or
Jim Beam® Double Oak Bourbon

a dash of Jim Beam® Bourbon
(optional) per drink

½ part sweet (red) vermouth

2 dashes Angostura® bitters
per drink

1 maraschino cherry per drink,
to garnish

★ Pour the bourbon, vermouth and bitters into a cocktail shaker. Add 2–3 ice cubes and shake vigorously for 30 seconds. Strain into a martini glass, garnish with a maraschino cherry and serve.

Old Fashioned

This smooth cocktail, with a hint of sweetness, brings out the very best in Kentucky bourbon. An Old Fashioned goes perfectly with meaty dishes such as burgers and steaks, so load up your glass with plenty of ice and enjoy it at a hot summer barbecue.

BUILD IN: Glass
MIX METHOD: Stir and build
SERVE IN: Tumbler

2 parts Jim Beam Black® Bourbon or Jim Beam® Double Oak Bourbon

a dash of sugar syrup per drink

a dash of orange bitters per drink

a dash of Angostura® bitters per drink

thin strip of pared orange peel per drink, to garnish

★ Half-fill a tumbler with ice cubes. Add the bourbon, then the sugar syrup and bitters, and stir for 1 minute until the ice begins to melt slightly and the ingredients are thoroughly blended.

★ Fill the glass with more ice cubes. Twist the strip of orange peel, add it to the cocktail to garnish, then serve.

Old Fashioned Kentucky Mud

Ever wondered what an Old Fashioned crossed with a Mississippi mud pie would taste like? Well, wonder no more! This sweet cocktail enhances the mixture of Jim Beam® Bourbon and Jim Beam® Honey by giving them a fantastic chocolate twist.

BUILD IN: Shaker
MIX METHOD: Shake and strain
SERVE IN: Small tumbler or small martini glass

1 part Jim Beam® Bourbon

1 part Jim Beam® Honey

½ part dark chocolate sauce

1 teaspoon crushed honeycomb (cinder toffee) or honeycomb chocolate bar (such as Crunchie) per drink, to garnish (optional)

★ Pour the Jim Beam® Bourbon, Jim Beam® Honey and chocolate sauce into a cocktail shaker. Add 2–3 ice cubes and shake vigorously for 30 seconds. Strain the cocktail into a small tumbler or martini glass, garnish with the honeycomb, if using, and serve.

Berries and Cream Beam

Cocktail or dessert? The Berries and Cream Beam straddles both, blending Jim Beam® Bourbon with raspberry liqueur, cream and a tried-and-tested partner – chocolate – for delicious results. Sweet and smooth, this tempting treat is for those who like their cocktails luxurious.

BUILD IN: Shaker
MIX METHOD: Shake and strain
SERVE IN: Martini glass

1½ parts Jim Beam® Bourbon

scant part Chambord® Liqueur

½ part dark chocolate sauce or dark crème de cacao

½ part double cream

pinch of drinking chocolate powder per drink, to garnish

★ Pour the bourbon, Chambord® Liqueur, chocolate sauce or crème de cacao and cream into a cocktail shaker. Add 2–3 ice cubes and shake vigorously. Strain into a martini glass. Sprinkle over the chocolate powder and serve.

Jim's Winter Cup

Perfect for those long winter nights, this is a warming hug in a mug. If you don't have a vanilla pod you can add a small splash (about ¼ teaspoon) of vanilla extract instead. For a fun garnish, serve with a cinnamon stick stirrer.

BUILD IN: Saucepan
MIX METHOD: Heat, stir and build
SERVE IN: Mug or heatproof glass

10 parts cloudy apple juice

a pinch of muscovado sugar per drink

1 cinnamon stick (about 5cm/ 2 inches long) per drink

½ vanilla pod (split lengthways) per drink

2 cloves per drink

1 whole star anise per drink (optional)

1½ parts Jim Beam Black® Black or Jim Beam® Double Oak Bourbon

To garnish

1 slice of lemon per drink

1 cinnamon stick per drink (optional)

★ Pour the apple juice into a small saucepan with the sugar and spices. Stir over a low heat for 3–5 minutes, ensuring the liquid does not come to the boil.

★ Take the pan off the heat and stir in the bourbon, then strain into a mug or heatproof glass. Add a slice of lemon and a cinnamon stick to stir, if using. Serve hot.

Tale of Two Beams

This drink can be described as an Irish coffee, Kentucky style. It's made by blending two different varieties of Jim Beam® (although, at a pinch, you can stick with one variety and increase the quantity accordingly), and mixing it with dark, bitter coffee. Be sure to use good-quality, freshly brewed strong coffee for maximum impact.

BUILD IN: Heatproof glass
MIX METHOD: Stir and build
SERVE IN: Heatproof glass

8 parts freshly brewed, hot filter coffee

a generous pinch of brown sugar per drink

1½ parts Jim Beam Black® Bourbon or Jim Beam® Double Oak Bourbon

2 parts double cream

½ part Jim Beam® Honey

★ Pour the hot coffee into a heatproof glass, stir in the sugar and the Jim Beam Black® or Jim Beam® Double Oak.

★ Whip the double cream with the Jim Beam® Honey in a small jug to very soft peaks. Be careful not to over-whip the mixture – you want a thick liquid, not whipped cream. Spoon the cream gently over the coffee, so that it floats on top, and serve.

Index

E

eggs
  cobb salad with blue cheese bourbon
    dressing 34
  eggs benedict with easy bourbon
    hollandaise 26
elderflower: Happy Hollow Hedgerow 156
English muffins: eggs benedict with easy
  bourbon hollandaise 26

F

fennel: Jim Beam® piri piri prawn skewers 45
feta cheese
  bourbon-roasted vegetables and cheese 99
  watercress and feta salad with honey
    dressing 36
fish
  bourbon-glazed salmon fillets 88
  pan-fried fish with burnt whiskey butter 90
  smoked salmon with pickled vegetables 30
fruit cake loaf 129

G

ginger: rhubarb and ginger upside-down
  cake 138
glaze, everyday bourbon 116
goat's cheese: bourbon-roasted vegetables
  and cheese 99
Grant, Ulysses S. 14
gravy, Jim's 84

H

ham
  Beam's baked ham 68
  eggs benedict with easy bourbon
    hollandaise 26
Happy Hollow Hedgerow 156
haricot beans: bourbon Boston beans 112
harissa: barbecue bourbon and harissa
  beef 74
harvest chilli with mixed beans 92–3
hazelnuts: watercress and feta salad with
  honey dressing 36
high wine 12–13
hollandaise, easy bourbon 26
honey dressing 36
hot dogs with onion chutney 51

I

ice cream
  Cherry Picker 169
  easy chocolate, bourbon and raisin ice
    cream 148

J

jalapeños: fully loaded black bean
  nachos 50
Jim Beam®
  history 12–15
  production 12–13
Jim Beam® Apple 18
  Apple & Maple Mule 160

Jim Beam Black® 16
Jim Beam® Bourbon 16
Jim Beam® cherry pie 133
Jim Beam® chicken nuggets 40
Jim Beam® Double Oak 17
Jim Beam® Honey 18
  Honey Beam Blush 161
  Old Fashioned Kentucky Mud 178
  Tale of Two Beams 180
Jim Beam® Maple Fizz 173
Jim Beam® Original 16
Jim Beam® pecan pie 124
Jim Beam® piri piri prawn skewers 45
Jim Beam® Rye 15, 17
Jim Beam® Vanilla 19
Jim's Mint Julep 158
Jim's Winter Cup 179
julep, Jim's Mint 158

K

kale: warm chicken Caesar salad 39
Kentucky bourbon chocolate shake 150
Kentucky carrot cake 126
Kentucky Manhattan 174
Kentucky quarter pounder 79
kidney beans: spiked chilli con carne 70

L

lamb: barbecued lamb skewers 82
lemons
  Jim Beam® Maple Fizz 173
  Long Lick Lemonade 170
  Sour Jim 162

R

radishes: smoked salmon with pickled vegetables 30
raisins: easy chocolate, bourbon and raisin ice cream 148
Red Stag by Jim Beam® 19
rhubarb and ginger upside-down cake 138
rice
    baked sweet and sour chicken thighs 83
    Bourbon and bacon risotto 62

S

salads
    Asian slaw 42
    cobb salad with blue cheese bourbon dressing 34
    warm chicken Caesar salad 39
    watercress and feta salad with honey dressing 36
salmon
    bourbon-glazed salmon fillets 88
    smoked salmon with pickled vegetables 30
salsa, sweetcorn 60
sauces
    bourbon barbecue dip 111
    bourbon mayonnaise 46
    easy bourbon hollandaise 26
    Jim's gravy 84
sausages: hot dogs with onion chutney 51
sesame seeds: roasted sesame noodles 86
skewers
    barbecued lamb skewers 82
    Jim Beam® piri piri prawn skewers 45
smoked salmon with pickled vegetables 30

smoky steak with bourbon butter 72
soup: butternut squash soup with chilli peanuts 28
sour cherries: bourbon cherry brownies 122
Sour Jim 162
soured cream
    cobb salad with blue cheese bourbon dressing 34
    fully loaded black bean nachos 50
    New York bourbon cheesecake 140
sparkling wine: Clermont Champagne 164
squash
    butternut squash soup with chilli peanuts 28
    roasted butternut squash 104
sweet and sour chicken thighs 83
sweet potatoes
    baked sweet potatoes 108
    harvest chilli with mixed beans 92
sweetcorn: pulled pork tacos with sweetcorn salsa 60
syrup, bourbon 24

T

tacos: pulled pork tacos with sweetcorn salsa 60
Tale of Two Beams 180
tarte tatin, bourbon pear 136
tomato ketchup: bourbon baby back ribs 64–5
tomatoes
    cobb salad with blue cheese bourbon dressing 34
    harvest chilli with mixed beans 92–3
    spiked chilli con carne 70
tortilla chips: fully loaded black bean nachos 50
truffles, bourbon chocolate 146

V

vegetables
    bourbon-roasted vegetables and cheese 99
    harvest chilli with mixed beans 92–3
    pickled vegetables 30
    see also carrots; sweet potatoes, etc
vermouth
    Bardstown Boulevardier 165
    Kentucky Manhattan 174

W

watercress and feta salad with honey dressing 36
wine: Clermont Champagne 164

Y

yogurt, whiskey baked apples with 139

Notes on the recipes

Standard level spoon measurement are used in all recipes.
1 tablespoon = one 15ml spoon
1 teaspoon = one 5ml spoon

Both imperial and metric measurements have been given in all recipes. Use one set of measurements only and not a mixture of both.

The cocktail recipes in this book have been based on a part being 25ml (1fl oz). If preferred, a different volume can be used, providing the proportions are kept constant within a drink and suitable adjustments are made where needed.

Eggs should be medium unless otherwise stated. The Department of Health advises that eggs should not be consumed raw. This book contains dishes made with raw or lightly cooked eggs. It is prudent for more vulnerable people such as pregnant and nursing mothers, invalids, the elderly, babies and young children to avoid uncooked or lightly cooked dishes made with eggs. Once prepared these dishes should be kept refrigerated and used promptly.

Pepper should be freshly ground black pepper unless otherwise stated.

This book includes dishes made with nuts and nut derivatives. It is advisable for customers with known allergic reactions to nuts and nut derivatives and those who may be potentially vulnerable to these allergies, such as pregnant and nursing mothers, invalids, the elderly, babies and children, to avoid dishes made with nuts and nut oils. It is also prudent to check the labels of pre-prepared ingredients for the possible inclusion of nut derivatives.

ABOUT
JIM BEAM®

SEVEN GENERATIONS, more than 200 years and just one goal:
to make the best bourbon in the world.

Today, Jim Beam® is the WORLD'S NO.1 BOURBON, enjoyed throughout
the world, from our hometown in Kentucky to every corner of the globe.
But we're far from an overnight success — founded in 1795, our passion
for making truly great bourbon has been passed down from generation
to generation.

A lot has changed in the 220 or so years since Jacob Beam sold his first
barrel of 'Old Jake Beam Sour Mash' whiskey, but we're proud to say
that things at Jim Beam® have remained more or less the same.
We still use the same key ingredients and the same basic process, aging
our bourbon in charred oak barrels for twice as long as the law requires
to ensure the perfect smooth flavour in every batch.

Nowadays, the Beam family has grown, and you can enjoy a range
of bourbons to suit your taste. But with all of our experience being
poured into every bottle, you know that you're enjoying
THE WORLD'S FINEST BOURBON.